By KATIE HEANEY

Never Have I Ever

Dear Emma

Public Relations (with Arianna Rebolini)

Would You Rather?

WOULD YOU RATHER?

WOULD YOU RATHER?

· · · · · · · · · ·

a memoir of
growing up
and coming out

Katie Heaney

BALLANTINE BOOKS  NEW YORK

A Ballantine Books Trade Paperback Original

Copyright © 2018 by Katie Heaney

Published in the United States by Ballantine Books, an imprint of Random House, a division of Penguin Random House LLC, New York.

BALLANTINE and the HOUSE colophon are registered trademarks of Penguin Random House LLC.

ISBN 978-0-399-18095-8

Ebook ISBN 978-0-399-18096-5

Printed in the United States of America on acid-free paper

randomhousebooks.com

2 4 6 8 9 7 5 3 1

Book design by Susan Turner

CONTENTS

WOULD YOU RATHER?

Dear Reader,

For most of my life I was boy crazy. I can remember every boy I liked all the way back to kindergarten. The only thing that seemed at all off was that, as of the age of twenty-six, I had yet to sleep with or date any of them. Until college, I told myself I was shy. A late bloomer. Besides, my parents had made it illegal for me to date before sixteen—and I was not the sort of teen who breaks the rules.

After college, I wasn't as sure what to tell myself anymore.

I did my best to explain myself in my first memoir, Never Have I Ever. *After it came out, I thought, my life would change. And in a way, I was right. While change didn't come easily (at all), or overnight, it did come, eventually, and looking very different than I imagined. Not that I ever felt I had a trustworthy imagination when it came to love. But what makes sense to me now was unimaginable to me even five years ago. Five years ago, I was so sure I knew myself completely. And yet, here I am, unpredicted.*

If you, too, are a person who has ever found herself Googling something like "is it normal if you've never had a relationship" or "can someone realize they're queer when they're kind of old" or "oldest living virgin," if you have ever wondered if it's normal not to feel normal—this one's for you.

xo, Katie

1

THE L WORD

The first time it occurred to me that I could be anything less than 100 percent straight, I was twenty-one. I was also in Spain, halfway into a semester abroad in Madrid, and I was not having a very good time.

There were one hundred students in my program. Most were American, from the East Coast, though there was also a not-insignificant contingent from Cuba and the Dominican Republic. On the flight over I'd entertained the vague possibility that I might finally find a boyfriend among the students I'd meet, and have one of those whirlwind study-abroad romances my friends kept having. Then I got there, and looked around the auditorium where we first gathered, and counted exactly seven men. Total. Two of whom, I later learned, were gay. Well, at least two.

A third was considered a very likely suspect, but nobody knew for sure. And then, within three days of touching down on foreign soil, the cutest of the five (or four) straight guys there found the girl who looked most like a sorority president, and she dumped her boyfriend back home, and the two of them commenced their whirlwind study-abroad romance, whose tumultuous nature would provide a kind of comforting *Real World*–esque entertainment for the rest of us. Seeing as the demographics really allowed for only one heterosexual high-drama study-abroad relationship, I immediately admitted defeat, and settled instead on finding lifelong best friends.

That mission didn't go much better. The closest I came was a trio of Penn State students who'd arrived in Madrid as a fully formed clique. I could rope them into a night out or—my preference—a daytime historical-site visit once in a while. But they were wealthier than me, and much bigger partiers than I was (not hard to be), and kind of bitchy. And I say that with the utmost admiration. I love mean people. It feels so good when a mean person likes you. It's like, *I guess I* am *extremely cool.* I basked in that glow for as long as they tolerated my mom-ish friend herding, which was maybe about a month.

My friendlessness coupled with my inability to afford travel outside the country, or eat out very much, meant I had a lot of time to myself. On weekend days I'd force myself into modest, repetitive adventure: I'd take a bus to Puerto del Sol to buy myself a cream Neapolitan at La Mallorquina and then window-shop and walk through Plaza Mayor. I'd make yet another trip to the Prado and visit my favorite paintings and write depressing journal entries. I have never been very good at open-ended explor-ing, and back then I was even worse. If I must do it I need at least one fixed destination, usually involving food, and once there, I can wander within a small, neat circumfer-ence of that spot. Before going anywhere alone I triple-check my routes, and usually I overestimate how long it will take me to get there. It isn't quite getting lost that I fear so much as it is the associated embarrassment—*looking* lost, or looking somehow out of place. Looking alone.

My guilt wouldn't allow me to wallow in my host's apartment all day every weekend, but it did not mind if I did so most weeknights after school. In the afternoons, at the end of my half-hour, humid, and mostly uphill walk home from the university, I would stop at the shop across the street to buy a Diet Coke and a little bag full of gummy candy, and then I'd head upstairs for the night. There I'd eat the late lunch my generous if curmudgeonly señora made daily for my roommate and me, though because my roommate had a life, I often ate for us both. And then, with three or four hours left before I could reasonably go to bed, I would watch TV.

There was no Netflix streaming at that time, so I ille-gally and painstakingly downloaded everything I watched one episode at a time. There was also no WiFi, so in order to do this I had to plug my laptop into the modem by an ethernet cord I stretched across the tiny living room to the dining-room table, where I sat to watch shows until my señora came home. She'd walk in around 6:00 each evening and, finding me sitting there, say, "*Ya estás.*" You're still here. Sometimes I'd wait a while before my

retreat, and we'd watch TV separately, together—me at
the table watching on my laptop with headphones on, eating gummies, her on the couch watching talk shows on
her 32-inch screen, eating a bowl of potato chips. Sometimes I'd head right for my room, my loneliness making
that kind of extended, quiet indifference to each other feel
intolerable. If I opened each episode of a show in its own
tab and it finished downloading all the way before I disconnected, I could watch it atop the scratchy IKEA comforter in my room. If it didn't finish, or an episode froze
up five minutes in—which happened a lot—I was devastated. Then I'd have to read or, worse, write more depressing journal entries.

First I worked my way through *The Office,* starting
again from the beginning. Then I re-watched the better
seasons of *Sex and the City* (two through four). Then I felt
like watching something I hadn't already seen—ideally
something with more than four seasons, so I knew it
might last me a significant portion of my remaining time
in Madrid. (Nothing soothes me like a long-term goal.)
And, with no social life of my own to speak of, I knew I
wanted something with lots of relationships and friendships and drama. Beyond these criteria I don't remember
exactly how it was that I arrived at *The L Word.* All I know
is that as soon as I started the pilot, I was hooked.

That's not to say the show was very good, which it
often wasn't. The music (to say nothing of the theme
song) was melodramatic, as was the plot. The characters'
behavior was frequently reprehensible, and their clothing,
insane. But almost all of those reprehensible characters
were women, and the less reprehensible ones (for nobody

on that show is truly innocent) were, too. My screen was full of women. Their omnipresence was striking. I couldn't believe that a show like this had ever aired. For multiple seasons. And yes, it was premium cable, and yes, everyone on it was skinny and beautiful and almost everyone was femme and white, and yes, it was so, so far from perfect. But it was also so, so different from everything I was used to.

I was (and am) used to watching shows and movies dominated by men and, secondarily, the women they sleep with. It's been more than ten years since the first episode of *The L Word* aired, and—aside from the rare exception, like *Orange Is the New Black*—that hasn't really changed. Women are one another's friends, sometimes, but mostly they are men's girlfriends and wives. In *The L Word,* every role was played by a woman: temptress café owner, millionaire philanthropist, sexy carpenter, failing novelist, famous athlete, closeted cougar wife, sex worker cum hairstylist, DJ. This world, in its forceful femaleness, was something that greatly appealed to me. I did not feel a part of it, but I found myself longing to be. Mostly, I thought, this was because I missed my own world of girls, carrying on our life together without me, back at school in Illinois. But it kind of seemed like there was something else going on, too.

That thing was Shane.

If you haven't seen the show, do yourself a favor and Google Image search "Shane McCutcheon" right now. I mean, look at her. Shane—played by Kate Moennig—is *The L Word*'s resident heartbreaker, an impossibly skinny, impossibly gorgeous jerk with disheveled hair the likes of which would suggest grave instability on anyone else's head. She's a womanizer, and a cheater, and possibly a moron, and yet she is so, so hot. There is her mouth—pouty lips always hanging open, the gravelly low voice that comes out of it. There are her fingers, bony and covered in silver jewelry. The first thing I distinctly remember her wearing was some sort of low-cut, lace-up leather halter crop top with leather pants slung so low you could see her pelvic bones. I was sort of like, *what the fuck is that outfit,* but I was also . . . intrigued.

Leather-halter-top incident aside, Shane was, by far, the most boyish lesbian of the bunch. I had never seen anyone like her. Back then, before I knew any better, I thought that the rest of the characters on the show could have just as easily passed for straight, but I didn't see how anybody could look at Shane and, for even a second, think she'd be interested in sleeping with men. She was usually dressed in muscle tees that highlighted her flat chest and lean, muscular arms, or else T-shirts under oversized blazers. She wore boots or sneakers but never heels or flats. Early on, there were also a lot of bad belts and arm cuffs, but you have to forgive her for that, because it was the early aughts, and everyone was accessorizing like there was no tomorrow. Shane was tall, too, always lifting girls' faces by the chin so she could kiss them. Often she had not yet spoken more than two words to these girls, but it didn't matter how implausible it was because everyone was happy—Shane, the girl she was kissing, and me, watching, invested enough in this character's sexcapades that I soon started to wonder if it "meant something."

It soon became imperative for me to know if the actress who played Shane was gay in real life, too. It was in the process of this online investigation—Googling as many variations on the search terms "Kate Moennig gay" and "Kate Moennig girlfriend" and "Kate Moennig sexuality" as I could think up—that I learned exactly how clichéd my fascination was. I found Web forums dedicated to this topic alone, and I clicked through dozens of pages, inhaling every bit of trivia (or baseless speculation) I came across. There were a number of Yahoo Answers posts written by straight girls wondering if their attraction to Shane meant they weren't so straight after all. ("Did Watching the L Word Make Me Bi?") There were T-shirts for sale that read "I'd Go Gay for Shane" across the chest.

At first it was comforting to know I was far from the only one with a Shane fixation. The more I read, the easier it was to decide that Kate Moennig was simply one of those people whom everybody, no matter their orientation, is attracted to. Knowing that there were a bunch of other self-identified straight girls who were crushing on the same actress as I was didn't strengthen my feelings; if anything, it diminished them. Having a crush on this woman in particular didn't mean much about my sexuality, the same way that finding *The Office* funny doesn't mean much about your sense of humor. It just meant I was a human being with an extremely popular opinion.

Still, I wrote a Facebook message to my best friend, Rylee, back home, under the auspices of catching her up on what I'd been doing (nothing) and how I'd been feeling (bad, sad). And, by the way, there's this random TV show I'm newly obsessed with. I can't remember exactly what I said, but I know it included something along the lines of "I think watching this show is making me turn into a lesbian." And then I attached a picture of Shane.

I love to present my concerns and insecurities as half-jokey hyperbole so that nobody can tell I am actually very serious and terrified. It's like I believe that if I make a joke about it, it can't come true. It is the same thing I do when I am at the doctor and I attempt to ingratiate myself with the nurse by "joking" about the fact that I think I have a brain tumor because I get headaches a lot. Rylee knows this about me, so, understandably, she took this confession with a pretty massive grain of salt. In her reply, she did all the right things. She asked me questions, told me that, no matter who I was attracted to, I was fine and normal, and told me she loved me.

She also wrote that she agreed, Shane was extremely hot, and even she would probably have sex with her, or at least make out with her for a little bit.

So maybe that was all it was. In her message Rylee asked if I thought I was attracted to other women, and I wrote back that I didn't know. She asked if I was still attracted to men, and I wrote that I was. But after I sent it I second-guessed myself. As a sort of unscientific experiment with myself, I walked around Madrid looking only at the women and none of the men. I stared at the prettiest ones, trying to deduce whether I looked because I was admiring someone pretty or because I was attracted. I felt that in the course of watching the show I had lost the ability to tell the difference. Maybe I had been so thoroughly exposed to women (by a single female-dominated TV show; as if!) as the only possible object of desire that I had suddenly lost the ability to feel otherwise—as if my previous heterosexuality had been, effectively, brain-washed out of me. Like, basically, what evangelical Christians argue can happen to youths exposed to LGBTQ culture had actually happened to me.

I knew this was ridiculous, and yet I could not let it go. With no one to talk to and nothing much I could bring myself to do, thinking was all that was left. In the best of times I am prone to overanalysis, but when I am lonely there is no limit to how far inward I can go. On the bus, in class, in my bed, waking up before my alarm went off, I tried to work through my sexuality like a mathematical theorem. If A = zero boyfriends thus far and B = number of times you rewound that Shane and Carmen sex scene, C = . . . maybe kinda gay. But then, if A = the dozens of real-life crushes on boys you've had and B = the zero real-life crushes on girls you've had, C = straight, probably. But then, but then.

One night, when I was about halfway into season four of *The L Word,* the episode froze. I tried downloading it from another site, but that one froze, too. So did the third. By then I was far enough into my trip that the end was in sight, and I think that's why it wasn't so hard to let go. That, and the fact that I'd worn myself out. *The L Word* wasn't "making me" gay, but it had inspired an existential crisis I was no longer interested in experiencing. So, instead, I went about making the most of my remaining time in Spain, doing all the things I maybe should have been doing all along but could only rarely bring myself to do. I went to see Guernica and cried. I went to the southern coast with my cool mean pseudo-friends for a long weekend. I ate all the things that had comforted me over those four months, knowing that eventually I'd miss them, that eventually I'd forget just how sad I'd been walking through the city alone to buy them. And then, finally, I went home.

That fall, at the beginning of my senior year in college, I had crushes on two boys at once. For me and my overly dedicated brain, that was a rare feat. One was a freshman (lol) and the other was a junior, and together they took up enough of my brain space to push aside whatever remaining Shane obsession I had. At least until my birthday, when Rylee bought me the fifth season of *The L Word* on DVD, and I watched it in two days, and I was as glued to Shane's face as ever.

I didn't know what—if anything—it meant, but, for the moment, I didn't want to care. When I moved home after graduation, I hid the DVDs behind a row of books on my shelf instead of putting them up front with my others. It wasn't that I thought owning them was wrong, necessarily, or even that owning them meant something definite about me; it was that they didn't fit in. It was that I worried their presence might require an explanation, and I did not have one.

Girl #1 I Probably Like-Liked, Now That I'm Thinking About It

Aliza, second through fourth grade. In the Catholic K–8 school I attended through the fourth grade, the way a girl got popular was to be more like the boys. Maybe that changed after I left, sometime after the girls turned thirteen and the uniform switched from unisex leggings to tartan skirts, but as children we placed a premium on tomboyishness: no jewelry (apart from a crucifix), no nail polish, no dolls. At recess, we played kickball, and Aliza was always the first girl chosen. She had white-blond hair and an ongoing flirtation with the most popular boy in our class mostly involving sports-based one-upmanship. Her circle was made up of the girls lucky enough to be both pretty and athletic. Occasionally, they did the charitable thing and loosened their standards. I remember sitting at their cafeteria table next to my best friend, Claire, being given our entrance exam. Aliza would say a city or a state, and we had to name as many sports teams that went with it as we could. You were allowed two strikes, and then you were out. Claire failed. Thanks to my father, I narrowly passed. My reward, as I recall it, was to be invited to all of their birthday parties. For a brief period I enjoyed the privileges of being one of Aliza's favorites, and so she invited me over after school. We played "Gangsta's Paradise" by Coolio on her parents' fancy stereo and sang along. The next year, when she started "going out" with the popular boy I was, unspecifiably, pissed.

else. Dark blond, almost the exact color of her skin. I
know it seems crazy, but she was the first person I'd really
looked at and thought, *Huh. That girl might be gay.*

What I knew for sure was that she dressed amazingly.
Not that the bar was particularly high in a Midwestern
public policy graduate program. But she vaulted leaps and
bounds above it. Some days she dressed tomboyishly—
ripped jean shorts and Chucks with an oversized button-
down shirt—and others she dressed more femme: a
sundress and espadrille wedges, a bandanna tied Rosie the
Riveter–style around her head. Our class met just once a
week, and Taylor seemed to miss at least a third of our
sessions. If we got more than five minutes into class and
she hadn't shown up, I'd feel let down. Then the weather
got colder and she started showing up in a leather jacket,
and I became more forgiving. Obviously, she had a lot of
cool things going on in her life.

My crush on Taylor was different from crushes I had
on boys. That much I knew. It felt even more theoretical,
even less worth doing something about. I did not picture
us holding hands, or kissing, or even really talking. I did
not envision a future in which we were girlfriends. I did
not obsess over her in the same way, or enter into the familiar cycle of nervous excitement, hope, frustration,
hope, anguish, disappointment. I just . . . noticed her.
And kept noticing her. And wondered, every time I saw
her, if she was gay. I liked looking at her. I wondered if it
was only that I wanted to look like her, and then I thought,
No, I'm pretty sure that's not it. But still, somehow, it didn't
feel real. I hoped that we would be put in the same discussion group at some point, but when we weren't, I was

never crushed. I told Rylee about her, but not in very much detail. It felt more like an inside joke than anything serious, like a "girl crush," devoid of any real sexuality. I presented it winkingly—like, isn't this funny, how I'm taken with this girl?—and so Rylee did not take it seriously, either. But I stared at Taylor far too much to play it off entirely as a joke to myself.

Anyway, it turned out she had a boyfriend. And, from the beginning of the semester to the end of the year, when I saw her on campus holding his hand, she slowly grew out that perfect haircut. So I forgot about her.

But then I got a crush on another short-haired girl I saw around school. We had no classes together, so I saw her almost never. She was short, with short, sandy-brown hair she tousled in the front and often tucked under a yellow beanie. She wore men's clothing—another revelation, another girl unlike any I'd ever seen in real life. For a long time I didn't know her name, so I (jokingly!) called her That Girl I'm In Love With. Then Rylee had a class with her and learned her name was Kristin.

When I talked about Kristin with Rylee, we had much the same conversation as when earlier moments of sexual confusion—over Shane on *The L Word,* or all the sensual lip-biting in Tegan and Sara's "Call It Off" video—had left me stressed and obsessive:

RYLEE: "Maybe you're just not one hundred percent straight. Most people probably aren't."
ME: "Yeah."
RYLEE: "I mean, I think plenty of girls are hot."
ME: "I know."

RYLEE: "Would you want to date her? If she were single, I mean."
ME: "I don't know. I can't picture it." (Of course, then, I couldn't really picture dating *anyone*.)
RYLEE: "Well, try not to worry about it. Just see who you like."

Rylee always made it abundantly clear that she would love me no matter who I was attracted to, and I knew that was the truth. But I also think there was a pattern to these discussions that made me come off like the girl who cried gay. Or, at least, that's how I felt each time I talked to one of my straight friends about it. Then I met Sheila.

It was in another class I can (surprise!) hardly remember, though I know the subject was feminist policy. I got there early the first day, and about ten minutes later, Sheila came in, and sat down next to me. I remember immediately wanting to know her. Half her head was shaved, and the rest of her thick, curly black hair was pulled into a high ponytail. She had tattoos up and down both arms and unshaved armpits. She wore red lipstick and a very short skirt. She said hi, I said hi back, and then we became friends in the typical shared-class trajectory: sitting by each other turned into walking to class together turned into studying together turned into saying hi at student happy hours. It was on one of those early walks to or from class—over a bridge with an insulated pathway to protect students from Minnesota winters—that Sheila told me she was queer.

Perhaps I should not have been scandalized, or surprised, but I was. While she was certainly not the first queer woman I had known, she became, in that moment, the first woman I knew *for certain* to be queer. That semester Sheila was reeling from a fairly recent breakup with a long-term girlfriend, and once I knew that, we entered my favorite phase of a new friendship—the one in which each person details their relationship history from start to finish, beginning with the most recent and working backward. (My half of the conversation was always much shorter, which is just as well, because I have always preferred to listen.) We were both single and frustrated—Sheila because (in her words) she needed to get laid, and I because (in my words) I was confused. In a roundabout sort of way I intimated my identity crisis to Sheila, hemming and hawing about how I wondered if it was possible, maybe, that I was not as straight as I'd always thought. When she asked the question "Well, how do you identify?," I realized I didn't know how to answer. Every real-life (and almost every celebrity) crush I'd had before that year had been heterosexual, and yet the word "straight" when applied to myself felt increasingly uncomfortable, like a shirt I'd grown out of but couldn't bring myself to discard. I suspected that I experienced more attraction to women than the average straight girl, but I wasn't sure that it was enough to "earn" any other label.

As soon as I started talking about sexuality to Sheila, I couldn't stop. It was different—easier and heavier all at once—than talking to Rylee about it. I confessed to her that I'd recently changed my OkCupid orientation to "bisexual" for a single night. I was on my third or fourth stint on the site at the time, and late one night, huddled over my laptop in my dark bedroom, I simply changed myself from a straight woman to a bisexual one. With a single click. I looked through a few profiles, more trying to imagine myself as someone who was genuinely appraising these women than actually feeling like I was that person. I felt clammy and self-conscious, and when I woke up the next morning I switched myself back to straight again. But from then on, Sheila considered me a queer person, and I let her.

Sometimes we'd talk about guys (she started dating one toward the end of the year), and that always felt natural. Sometimes we'd talk about girls, and that did not. One spring afternoon near graduation we sat on a sunshiny bar patio with Rylee. We talked about finals, and graduation, and then about two of Sheila's female friends, who were going to meet up with us.

"Are they cute?" I asked. (I was on my second margarita.)

Immediately, I was embarrassed. I felt like I was playing a character—a young metropolitan woman at ease with her fluid, freewheeling sexuality. It seemed transparently disingenuous. Especially with Rylee there—Rylee, who had comforted me through so many failed heterosexual crushes. I felt like a fraud. Surely nobody bought me as an actual queer person—not even I did.

"They're cute," Sheila said, nodding, and I let the subject drop. It was one thing to talk about sexuality as a theoretical possibility. But, as usual for me, the moment other people became potentially involved, I wanted to run away from both them and myself. I wanted to sink into the earth. Rylee and I went home before the cute friends even showed up.

The day we graduated was hot and underwhelming. I wore the same dress I'd worn to my college graduation, three years earlier. As it always does on days when I expect a lot from it, my hair under-performed. I wore flat sandals so that when I walked across the stage to accept a diploma I was already starting to regret signing up for, I wouldn't trip. After the ceremony, we took family and friend photos on the lawn outside. I posed with Rylee. I posed with Sheila, too. And then, ten hours later, we made out.

What happened was: we drank too much. What happened was, the graduating class went out to celebrate that night at a bar. I changed from my floral Anthropologie dress into an electric blue one that static-clung to my legs and made it difficult to walk at the speed to which I am accustomed. I don't remember much of being out that evening, but I do remember walking home through campus, me and Rylee and Sheila and this guy Devin, deciding to take a "shortcut" through several interconnecting buildings that would kick us out on the street opposite ours. We walked past the business building, through economics, and into political science, opening the door to the descending stairwell outside the library. Once we were on the stairs, someone—and, knowing her, I'm nearly positive it was Rylee—said, "I always wanted to make out with someone in this stairwell." I was first to the bottom of the stairs, turning to say that I'd once walked through a couple's fight in that stairwell, when Sheila pushed me against the wall and kissed me. Rylee hollered and Devin laughed nervously. Because Sheila really went for it, and because I was drunk, and because I was yet again graduating from another era of my life with the sense that I didn't have all that much to show for it apart from five digits' worth of debt, I went for it, too.

"Jeez," said Devin.

"But *I* still didn't get to!" said Rylee.

I pulled away, laughing, and we pushed open the door, emerging outside the conference room where Rylee and I had once been scolded for taking cookies off a refreshment table meant for the people meeting inside.

"It pays to be queeeeeer," sang Sheila. She took my hand in hers and swung it back and forth. Kissing her had felt more or less like the other few times I'd drunkenly and sexlessly kissed my female friends at frat parties in college, the way straight girls sometimes do when you're drinking at a party and you know boys are watching and it feels important to know you are capable of turning them on. For show. Kissing Sheila was a performance. I squeezed her hand anyway, and we left the building to walk toward home.

I went to bed just sober enough to wonder how I'd feel the next morning, sure that I would feel different/grown up/changed/clearer for having kissed an actual queer person. To my disappointment, I didn't. I'd found no easy solution to the problem of me. All I had was another name on the fairly short list of people I'd kissed without feeling what I knew I was supposed to when it counted.

I fell in love with a small university in central Illinois, approximately an eight-hour drive from my parents' house. Throughout college my plan always was to return to Minnesota, and I spent much of that time trying to brainwash my new Illinois friends into thinking they might want to live there, too. (It was cheaper than Chicago, I reasoned, and much less bro-y, and everyone was so nice, and so tall . . .) Six months after we graduated, living with our parents and working menial jobs we hated, Rylee and I decided we missed being in school and figured we should just go back. We both wanted to study public policy, so I immediately began the hard sell on the graduate program at the University of Minnesota. We applied, we got in, and she moved from the Chicago suburb where she was living with her parents. *I did it,* I thought. Thus began what I expected to be the rest of our lives in Minnesota.

Rylee and I lived in Minneapolis together for three years. For the first, we lived in a fake-fancy apartment built for students, most of them undergrads, paying almost twice as much as we should have because it had a gym we'd use once and because it was across the street from where most of our classes were held. When that lease was up, we made the move to a building farther from school but half as expensive. It took us maybe twenty minutes to walk to class every day, but most Minnesotans aren't in the habit of commuting by foot, especially in the winter. But I found I enjoyed the forced mind-wandering these walks provided, and I soon started coming up with little story ideas on the way to and from school. There were seven or eight blogs and websites I read religiously around this time, and, at some point, it occurred to me that maybe I could write for one of them.

That summer, during break, I submitted a story I'd written to my favorite website at the time, *The Hairpin*. The site mostly featured writing from young women who hadn't been published before (one of whom would later become my first roommate in New York), and this made it seem possible that I could be one of them. I hadn't intended to make a habit of writing, really, but when the piece was published, and I saw my name in print and read all the nice comments, I got addicted. I started writing more, for other sites, too, and then a literary agent emailed me, and suddenly I was working on a book. As a result, I spent most of my second year of grad school mentally checked out. I didn't want to network or go to talks or do any of the other things my classmates were doing to try to get policy jobs. I wanted to write. I could have quit the program and saved myself a year of debt, but I knew I shouldn't count on writing as a career. Finishing school was the practical thing to do, so I did it.

After we graduated, Rylee and I moved into an almost comically charming apartment complex in South Minneapolis—old brick buildings covered in ivy, surrounding a courtyard lined by hedges and gardens. There was no central air and the heating was furnace-only (unusual in Minnesota), and no dishwasher, but otherwise, it was perfect. We intended to stay there until one of us met a man worth moving in with. And we both had every reason to believe that it would be Rylee—she didn't have a boyfriend at the time, but it was pretty much the first time in our friendship that she hadn't. I, on the other hand, had never had one at all. I bought the heaviest desk I could buy, a sturdy wood thing almost six feet long and over two feet deep, deposited in my room by the two biggest men I'd ever seen in my life. It was a very, very heavy desk; it wasn't going anywhere, so neither was I. This was where I would work on my book, which went out to publishers shortly after I graduated. I maintained a halfhearted search for policy jobs while waiting to see if my book would sell, hoping somehow it would work out so I didn't have to get one.

It worked out. My agent called me one morning to tell me that someone (two someones, even!) wanted to buy my book. I was more relieved than excited (though I was that, too): I didn't have to get a government job. I'd been right to spend a full school year working on a book that could have gone nowhere. I could make a living from writing— for now, anyway.

Rylee soon got a job that let her work from home, too, and together we expressed a lot of good intentions about how we would structure our days: We would be at our desks from 8–4 or 9–5, breaking for a lunch we'd prepare together, to save money on groceries. When we were done we'd work out, and then we would hang out with other friends at their apartment or a bar. I'd spent most of my young life hoping I'd end up in a situation like this one, living with my best friend, both of us single, starting our actual adult lives together. I'd always thought I wanted my world to be smaller: my friends close, my job close, my social life at home. Any and all boyfriends existed somewhere nebulous outside this perfect little universe, if at all. It occurs to me now that what I wanted was a partner.

And for a while, living with Rylee was almost like having one. We did grocery shop together, and eat lunch together, and often work together across the dining-room table. Working at home turned out to be a challenge, however, since we suffered from similarly powerful mixtures of Catholic and Midwestern and strict-parent guilt and both felt ashamed and unproductive if we weren't constantly working. So we tried to help each other feel okay about working until 2:00 or 3:00 instead of 5:00 or 6:00. On weekends we took day trips around the state and occasionally hung out at parties at our friend Colleen's dental school fraternity for as long as we could stay awake. We settled into the kind of rituals other domestic partners share: a pizza night (Thursdays, frozen Jack's), a distribution of chores, a shared TV show to watch two episodes of together before bed. For a little while I really, truly loved it. This is the kind of environment I'm built to thrive in: a rut. Or so I thought.

Because after a while, even I got bored, and boredom makes me depressed. First I stopped getting dressed in the mornings, because what was the point? The only human I saw most days was Rylee, and she wasn't getting dressed anymore, either. Then I stopped working at my desk, because as beautiful as it was, it was not as comfortable as my bed. Around 3:00 or 4:00 in the afternoons I would change into workout clothes. But instead of going for a run or a walk outside, I got my exercise in the form of thirty-minute Jillian Michaels DVDs in the living room. Then I would shower and put my pajamas right back on again to make dinner, which I ate in front of the TV. The next day I would do the same. This is how I got through thirteen seasons of *Law & Order: SVU* in less than a year.

I didn't allow myself to recognize that I was unhappy, at first. It didn't make sense. I had wanted to live in Minnesota after college, and that's exactly what I was doing. I had wanted to live with Rylee, and here we were. I wasn't seeing much of anybody else, but I couldn't think of many other people I cared to see. Even after I bought my own car, I couldn't really think of anywhere to go. The person I liked hanging out with most was right here; why go anywhere else?

Mixed in among those indistinguishable days there were still some of the most comforting and most challenging evenings of my life, just talking to Rylee. I am sure other friends have influenced my character and my decision-making, but none so profoundly as her. We have been friends since we were eighteen; I haven't been an adult without her. Neither of us is particularly religious, but we are spiritual insofar as it serves the story of us: we are soul mates, deliberately placed by some mysterious force on opposite sides of the same dormitory floor. And now, here we were, in the living room in our perfect apartment, each of us curled up on the couches we'd wordlessly claimed as our own. It never mattered how much we'd talked about something before; there was always a few hours' worth more to be said. When we agreed about something, which was usually the case, I felt stronger, less alone. When we disagreed, which happened often earlier in our friendship and less as time went on, I felt angry, as determined I was right as she was. Then whatever it was would come up again, and I'd still disagree, but a little less stringently than before. Before I knew it, I had grown.

When friends of ours joked that it was as if Rylee and I, spending our nights together in front of the TV, were married, they were not wrong. And they did not mean it in a nice way. They meant that we were thirty-years-in-and-sexless married. They meant we were codependent-homebodies-who-ate-dinner-at-5:00-p.m. married. At first it was funny, an exaggerated joke, but over time it seemed truer and truer, and it started to bother us both. We really weren't going out very much. We weren't dating anyone. We were twenty-six years old. We were not ready to have the lives of seventy-year-old retirees yet. Ten months or so into our life in that beautiful apartment, I looked around—at the job I could do from my bed, the roommate who was also my best friend—and I realized that I could very easily keep living like this, here, with her, for the rest of my life. There was nothing in the foreseeable future that was going to change any part of it. For the first time in my life, I had the stasis I'd always wanted. And that scared the shit out of me. So when I sold my first book, and my agent and new editor suggested I think about making a trip to New York to meet them in person, it seemed like a sign. I had never given New York much thought before then, and didn't particularly expect to like it. But I needed to do *something* different, even for just a few days. I asked

Rylee if she'd like to come with me, and she said sure.
Then I asked if it was okay if we took the train. She
paused . . . "From here?"

Let me explain. I was perfectly fine with flying until I was
nineteen. That spring, I flew to China for a three-week
trip with a college class, and on the way over I stood by a
window at the back of the plane and gaped at the endless,
brilliantly white ice stretching out below us as we crossed
over the North Pole. The way back was different. Soon
after takeoff, the plane began to shake. Turbulence does
not begin to describe it. This felt as if a pair of giant hands
was slapping us back and forth between them. And then,
occasionally, we'd plummet. Or so it felt. After one particularly bad jolt, people began to pray and to cry. The
voice of the flight attendant came over the speaker, shouting, "Everyone, *stay in your seats!*" She sounded afraid, and
if *she* was afraid, I figured that couldn't be good. I clasped
my friend Aimee's hand tightly, and as we dipped again,
my life flashed before my eyes. I remember thinking: *I
can't believe that actually happens.*
　　Eventually, after what felt like at least an hour, the
"turbulence" stopped. I have no idea how much time actually passed. I only know it was enough to traumatize
me. The rest of the flight was perfectly, eerily smooth. I
overheard a woman sitting in the row behind mine tell her
neighbor that she'd been praying with a beaded bracelet a
monk gave her during her visit to the Shaolin Monastery.
The implication, I think, was that we owed her our lives.
　　From then on, if I could get somewhere without a plane,

I would. And if a friend proposed taking a trip to some-where accessible only by plane, I would invent a reason I couldn't go. I pretended it was a matter of preference. I have always liked traveling by train or car. When I was a kid, my family vacations were mostly road trips—we'd drive two or three days from Minnesota to Glacier National Park, Mon-tana, or Washington, D.C., or Tucson, Arizona, staying there a few days and then driving back. I remembered these trips as opportunities to eat lots of fast food and buy those little velvet pouches of pink and green rocks, but also to stare out the window and do absolutely nothing. And be-cause I have never really been able to justify doing nothing when I am not in transit, I have always appreciated having relaxation forced upon me. True, the longest time I'd trave-led nonstop previously was fourteen hours, and true, the train ride from Minneapolis to New York, via Chicago, would be thirty-six. But that would include sleeping.

Or so I thought, until we were actually on the train. The lights went out, and I reclined my seat as far back as it would go, pulled up the little leather seat extender, and stretched out. My legs dangled uncomfortably a good eight inches off the end. Rylee glared at me from the seat next to mine. I was okay up until hour thirty; it was the last six that really did me in. You get to a point where you think you're close to the city because you can see it, but what you do not realize is that it will take you two hours to creep along that final stretch, your legs starting to hurt from the nonstop restless bouncing.

But somehow we got there. And I hated it, just like I thought I would. We caught a cab to the Chelsea studio apartment we were renting for our four-day stay along with our friend Joyce, who'd come up from med school in Philadelphia. My first thought upon walking through the front door was that the place had, somehow, seemed a lot bigger in the photos. We'd chosen it because it was centrally located and close to the *BuzzFeed* offices, where I had a part-time writing contract and planned to visit once or twice while I was there. We also chose it, I think, because "Chelsea" is one of the New York neighborhoods that people who don't live in New York and have never been can readily name. It seemed glamorous, or something. But being in that apartment and, later, walking around to find dinner, I felt underwhelmed. As someone who lives in any other part of the country, you see New York depicted so often and so prettily that it's hard not to get there, take one look around you, and think: *This is it?*

Then, too, everyone living in New York seemed obsessed with the fact that they lived in New York, and I found their smugness incredibly obnoxious. Obnoxious, despite the fact that the only real difference between New York City pride and Minnesota pride is that the former has three million more people and all of pop culture backing it up. Like many Midwesterners who do not hear their home states referenced much outside the context of their major-league sports teams, I was born on the defense, and had an outsize territoriality because of it. How dare anyone call my home state "flyover country"? How could so many people possibly think that they lived in the best place in the world when, in fact, *I* lived in the best place in the world?

When I first went to New York it was partly with the

goal to prove myself right—the city wasn't for me, and never would be. I already lived where I was meant to be and where I was sure I'd always want to stay: Minnesota. And when I got home, I felt safe.

But a year later, I went back to New York. Once again I took the train all the way out, but this time, I did so knowing that I could not, and would not, take the train back home. I was going out to take an intensive course of exposure therapy for my fear of flying at Hofstra University, and write about it for *BuzzFeed*. And at the end of this course, I would fly home. This time I knew enough to stay on the Lower East Side instead of Chelsea. But between the noise from the street outside and the fear of what awaited me at the end of the week, I hardly slept.

Each morning that week I took the subway to Penn Station and got on the Long Island Railroad out to the Hofstra campus, where two psychology grad students tried to scare me out of my fear of flying—the theory being that the more you are exposed to the stimulus that scares you, the less power it will have over you. The thing you're most afraid of is not actually the thing itself but the way you imagine it. Avoiding your fear only makes it loom larger, so you must confront it as much as possible. Fair enough, but what a terrible way to spend a week.

I spent most of the first two days strapped into a beat-up old airplane chair that shook when the virtual-reality program strapped to my head took my make-believe flights through a thunderstorm. When I was not in the headset, I was instructed to close my eyes and describe imaginary plane crashes in great detail. By the end of each session I felt drained and dull, and would find myself walking through Penn Station with little memory of how I'd gotten there. Still, I went out every evening after I got back to the city, reanimated by the open-endedness of every warm May night. It helped that I had a crush—not just on the one person in particular (more on that later), but also on everyone I met. Something had shifted between my first trip to New York and my second. My career was there. My people—my creative, brilliant, sardonic, Internet-obsessed people—were there. I did not know many of them very well yet, but there was so much possibility. Little by little, my life had moved to New York without me.

At the end of the week I got on a plane for the first time in four years and flew back to Minneapolis. My student therapists took me to the airport, and before I went through security, I told them that if, after all this, my plane crashed, I would haunt them for the rest of their lives. By then they knew me well enough to know that making jokes was how I coped with my terror.

I was nervous, but less nervous than I expected to be. My sense of responsibility finally outstripped my fear. The therapists told me I couldn't take Xanax, and I shouldn't watch a movie or read a book, either, if I could help it. The point was to not distract myself, to sit still with my fear, to accept it as a part of my life that could not, itself, hurt me. I still closed my eyes, and gripped my armrests when it got bumpy. But I was also exhausted—by the therapy, by my fear, by the amount of time I'd let pass without forcing myself to do something brave.

By the time I got on that plane, I'd decided that if I was really going to do this big, scary thing I'd been afraid of for more than four years, I might as well commit to confronting another one, too: I would leave home, and my best friend with it. When my new friends teasingly asked me when I was moving to New York, I picked a date just four months out: September, I said. I was surprised to find I meant it. The part of me that hoped I would die in a plane crash after all, just so I wouldn't have to go through with it, was, I assure you, very small.

4

I WANT TO BELIEVE

When I moved to New York in the fall, I left behind my bed, my desk, my dresser. I stashed boxes of my belongings in Rylee's storage unit and in my parents' basement. I did not think of this as a very big favor, because they would be there only a year. I was thinking of my move as less of a *move*-move and more a yearlong work abroad. That was the plan, initially: stay a year, then go home. I fit what I thought I'd need into eight medium-sized boxes and shipped them to my new apartment on the Lower East Side of New York, and then I got on a plane and went. It was the easiest flight I'd had in years because I was too excited to think about dying.

I was going to move into a new apartment, with a new

roommate—Chiara, a fellow *Hairpin* writer I'd become a big fan of, who already lived in New York. We'd met only once in person, on my last trip to the city, but we talked online almost every day. I'd found her email address several months back and written her a gushy note about her work. She'd replied immediately, equally generous in her use of exclamation points. Within a few days, we were great friends.

When I posted a picture of my New York apartment on Instagram, to announce my move and to brag, people gushed and cooed. I had not yet seen the apartment in person myself; I edited and filtered a photo Chiara had sent me. Over the month we'd been looking, she'd seen three or four places and fallen for this one. I'd seen the listing online and the pictures she sent me, and I had her word that it was really very nice. "It's pretty small, though," she kept saying. And I kept saying "Sure," like I understood. All I could see were the wood floors, the bright windows (the skylight!), the exposed brick walls I knew were coveted because I'd heard people say "exposed brick walls" on TV shows about New York. The rent, while more than twice what I'd been paying in Minneapolis, was, I was told, very good for the area. *So it's small*, I thought. It was only for a year.

Then I got there, on a very hot day at the very end of August, and when I saw my room I laughed. I lay down on the floor with my feet pressed against the door and reached my arms above me, touching the opposite wall. This was the longer side; I could not lie fully extended the other way. For the first few days I slept on the futon Chiara brought from her previous place, a gray-brown thing that was more like two slabs of fabric-covered metal rods stuck together than a piece of furniture in its own right. But I didn't mind.

In the mornings I had an office to go to, which was very welcome after almost a year spent working in sweatpants from my bed. In my first week I took the wrong subways in the wrong directions at least four times and cried because of it twice. That first week, before I'd bought a bed, we had a housewarming/welcome–to–New York party, and sixty or seventy people crammed into our 400-square-foot, air conditioner–less apartment. The man I was interested in—the one I'd liked since my last stint in New York, when I decided to move there— eventually showed up, alone, with a bottle of wine, after I worried he wouldn't come at all, and so did many of my new friends. I got so giddily drunk I sprayed a bottle of red wine on the wall in the process of opening it, leaving stains that were still there when I moved out. When it got too hot and too crowded, we went up to the roof to spread out and cool down, and even though I'd had a hard first week, I felt that I was where I was supposed to be.

That feeling lasted, unchallenged, for all of five or six months—as long as it took for me to meet all my Internet friends for drinks once, to get over the novelty of taking the subway to work, to realize exactly how much money I was spending, to see all the major museums I wanted to see, to start dating and promptly get dumped by the man I had thought, I'm embarrassed to say, would be the new boyfriend to go with my new life.

It's just as well he wasn't, since my new life turned out to be incredibly cramped.

My sixth-floor walk-up apartment on the Lower East Side in New York was so small I had to take my closet door off the hinges so that my IKEA double bed could fit in my room. In the summer I lay in bed sweating, and in the winter I froze, woken every night by a radiator that clanked and hissed almost pornographically, but did not produce any real heat. Outside my apartment I felt over-stimulated and antsy, but inside it I felt trapped. Despite the fact that I'd moved to New York determined to stay a Minnesotan—I refused to get a New York driver's license and swore I'd vote absentee—I'd still moved to this new city to change my life. To experience discomfort so that I might become something I couldn't otherwise have been. I'd achieved the first part, but I still felt the same.

I also felt guilty about having abandoned Rylee. That's what it felt like I'd done, at least. Never before in our friendship had she been the one left behind; our dynamic until then had been closer to that between sisters—my needy, less experienced one to her wiser free spirit. I think we both always assumed that if our friendship grew strained, she would be the one doing the tugging. I know I loved her more in the early years of our friendship than she loved me. But I also know that no friend has ever loved me as much as she did, even then. And for that, I felt I owed her my life. I assumed I'd always want to be there for her—physically present, the first on the scene. This was what I thought it meant to be someone's best friend when I was young: unwavering, selfless, perma-nent. My sense of duty is so ingrained that if it weren't for all the fear and physical weakness, I'd have made a perfect Marine.

But after eight years of friendship, the dynamic between Rylee and me had shifted. She helped me become a person who could move away from her. Still, being away from her wasn't easy. Especially once it was clear that some of the people I'd thought would become good friends of mine in New York wouldn't; in fact, some of the people who had seemed close to me, watching from the Internet back in Minnesota, weren't even good friends with one another. People had their own lives. I hadn't had much of one before I moved, but a few months in, after my brand-newness had mostly worn off, it was hard to remember why I'd been so sure that moving across the country would make it easier to get one.

It was around this time that I started reading my horoscope every day, off an app I downloaded because cool women on the Internet were tweeting about it. And then I downloaded another one, too, using one set of predictions to moderate the other. It was the first thing I did when I woke up in the room I hated. And for a while, reading my horoscope gave me hope that my life could still change for the better without any more effort on my part. I'd drained my savings to move across the country and live in a box; wasn't that enough?

The spring after I moved to New York, a pair of astrologers told me I was going to marry an older man from another country. As it happened, a few nights earlier I'd attended a singles' mixer for people obsessed with death (ostensibly for work), and had given my card to a handsome thirty-eight-year-old man from Argentina. We'd met during the icebreaker portion of the evening—an uncomfortable endeavor in any setting but, I assure you, never more so than at a singles' mixer at a morbidity museum. Pretty much everyone there was a goth, a funeral director, a tattooed Wiccan, a taxidermist, or all of the above. It didn't take me long to identify the only other person there with a sense of humor about the unusual circumstances in which we found ourselves: he was seated across the table from me, and he was cute. As instructed, we asked each other to explain the icebreaker words written on the labels stuck to our chests. I'd written "spectrophilia" (a sexual fetish for ghosts) on mine and, having been asked to explain it three times by then, regretted it immensely. His name tag read "baby bird," and when I asked why, he told me that he'd saved one that morning. He'd named it Kowalski—because, he said, every wounded soldier you root for in a war movie is named Kowalski. I found this very funny, only partly because I was drunk.

This guy was friends with one of the women running the event, and this, in my eyes, made him normal. Sure, we were both there, but only ironically. When one of the hosts climbed up onto a table and ordered everyone to participate in trivia, we stood side by side, rolling our eyes at the dork in the top hat who shouted his every answer. We refilled our plastic wine cups together and made small talk about what we each did for work. When I told him I was a writer, hence my attendance at this event, he said he'd be sure to look out for my story. I'd spent twenty-seven years on Earth without having ever given anyone my business card for flirting purposes. This seemed as good an opening as I'd ever get. I pulled one from my wallet and handed it to him, trying to make it clear that I wanted him to contact me if he was interested, while still acting vague enough for plausible deniability if he wasn't. He took my card, smiled, and put it in the pocket of his shirt. Soon after that, I waved goodbye and left.

Three days later, I met the astrologers. A co-worker and I had arranged for them to visit our office and read our star charts for an article. I loved them both immediately. They were warm, smiley, and just enough older than me that I was ready to believe just about anything they might tell me. They read my co-worker's chart first. She was visibly impressed, which, despite my determination to stay objective, made me giddy with excitement for my own reading. When it was my turn, they told me some things I already knew about myself (that I'm a Sagittarius, Leo rising; that I'm a hard worker who likes structure; that I like socializing but prefer small groups) and some that I didn't know but would certainly love to believe (that I was destined for great career success; that I was very independent, largely because I'd endured several long and dramatic romances in my past life; that I was a born leader). Then, finally, we got to the part I most cared about, the thing I always skimmed around for whenever I read my horoscope online: love.

The astrologers told me that I was "somewhat of a late bloomer," and I laughed in a way that indicated that that was a pretty big understatement. They asked for a few details about my relationship history, which did not take long to summarize. Then, they told me that my chart showed me becoming involved in a whirlwind romance with an older man—probably ten, fifteen years older, and likely from a foreign country.

"Oh my god," I said. My co-worker, who knew about the man from the singles' mixer, gasped.

"Does that ring true?" one of the astrologers asked.

"Well, I gave my number to a thirty-eight-year-old from Argentina a few nights ago," I said. He hadn't texted, or called, but surely there was no way that he could meet such specific criteria and not be the person the astrologers were talking about.

"I think you'll be hearing from him," they said.

He did not text me.

Or call.

Or email.

I was disappointed—less so in his failure to contact me than in the revelation that the astrologers' tidy, romantic love story wouldn't come true for me after all.

That should have been enough to end my love affair with astrology, but it wasn't. So many years spent reading incorrect and deliriously over-optimistic horoscopes in the backs of *Teen Vogue* and *CosmoGirl* magazines as a preteen hadn't stopped me from picking the habit back up in my late twenties, either. I excused the faulty parts of every forecast I read (the astrologers hadn't said *which* handsome older man, or *when* we'd become involved), and held on only to those predictions that were eventually proven true, or true enough. Astrology made me an avowed practitioner of confirmation bias—the tragically human tendency to seek out information that confirms one's beliefs while rejecting all information that challenges them.

I was particularly attached to *Astrology Zone,* an astrology site written by the enigmatic Susan Miller. Her forecasts were long and full of strangely specific details, which, while frequently unrelatable (Miller seems to believe we are constantly having elegant dinner parties and flying first class and negotiating movie-rights contracts), made those details that did ring true seem somehow more authentic. Often she filed her horoscopes three or five days late, and so I would start each month feeling lost. When my horoscope finally appeared, I'd read it still in bed, scanning quickly through it on my phone with one eye closed as if to protect myself from any prediction that might sound remotely negative. Still, even a mediocre horoscope was better than no horoscope at all.

It's probably not a coincidence that my favorite part of every horoscope was the least accurate thing about them—the love predictions, and the days listed as "Most Romantic Dates," of which there were usually ten or twelve. Which is absurd. That is almost half a month. With the possible exceptions of newlyweds on their actual honeymoon, and brand-new, five-day-old couples in their honeymoon phase, nobody has that much capital-r Romance each month.

Still, these dates planted themselves into my mental calendar, and if by chance something romantic(-ish) did happen on one of them, I was both immensely pleased and insufferably smug, telling a friend, "I *knew* this was coming." I should note that, in the grand tradition of molding one's life to fit the details provided by someone claiming psychic foresight, "something romantic," by my definition, could mean anything from Tinder-matching with someone I found cute to receiving a Gchat message that two of four friends polled found "mildly flirtatious." During my first two years in New York, the number of actually-kinda-romantic days I had would fit on one hand. Forget about the pinkie, I didn't need it. But Susan Miller's certainty that I was having a veritable romance-fest each and every month made my non-romantic life seem more, well, romantic. It made me feel like I was constantly on the verge of great love by simply living. It made love feel like my destiny, not something I had to actually go after. All of this is to say, it made me a little bit passive.

When someone I'd expressed interest in didn't text me back, I could find a reason for it in my horoscope. I chose not to be bothered by the passage of yet another Valentine's Day, because Susan Miller told me that my personal Valentine's Day would happen the week after. (It didn't, but I still bought a basketful of clearance Russell Stover marshmallow hearts for myself, like a *Cathy* comic, and hid them away in my refrigerator.) When I decided to break my Manhattan lease early and move to a new apartment with another friend in Brooklyn, I found support in an Astrology Zone forecast that told me that the position of the planet Saturn ensured I would not regret any housing-related decisions I made at that time.

It is probably my insatiable appetite for certainty that most attracted me to astrology. Because I have always wanted to believe. In God, in ghosts, in karma, in UFOs. I used to think I was the type of impressionable person who'd make perfect prey for a cult leader. In any cult documentary, before things turn tragic, there is a period in which the members are unreservedly blissed-out, high on their devotion. They are certain they are taken care of. That is how I want to feel all the time. For most of my life, I've wanted to believe things are out of my hands, and that my life is going to happen to me whether I take charge of it or not.

Soon after I moved to Brooklyn, though, I stopped seeking astrological validation. It took me almost two years in New York, but I realized my horoscopes had never really gotten anything meaningful right. Reading them made me more anxious than hopeful. And I was hard enough on myself without needing to feel like a disappointment if the month of April wasn't as magical for me as Susan Miller said it would be. That spring, I was ready to let go of some pressure, and outer space seemed like a good place to start.

I finally realized the planets had had little, if anything, to do with my move to Brooklyn, or my move to Manhattan before it. These were decisions I had made all alone. It had taken time for them to feel right, but finally they did. In making them I had proven to myself that I could be trusted with my own future. I knew more than I gave myself credit for. As far as I could tell, I was alone in the universe. But there were worse places to look for answers than within myself.

Girl #2

Kelly, summer after fifth grade. Kelly was from Northern Ireland and came to stay with my family as part of an exchange program that placed Protestant kids in Catholic homes and Catholic kids in Protestant homes to show them that here in America, it was possible for different religions to coexist peacefully. (As long as they are both Christian.) Though she was my age, Kelly seemed at least three years older, with a boyfriend named Stephen who sent her off to America with a teddy bear and a mixtape. She taught my brothers and me a number of Northern Irish slang terms that, in hindsight, were completely made-up, and she told my family that because of a fall she'd had as a baby, whenever she pressed her nose, she burped. In the basement where we shared a room, we played doctor. When I lifted her lime green Limited Too T-shirt to wrap the surgical blanket around her torso, I looked at her breasts for just a beat too long.

5

NEVER HAD I EVER

I wrote my first book with the complete confidence of someone who has never written a book. I don't think that's necessarily a bad thing; *Never Have I Ever* wouldn't have turned out the way it did had I really been able to imagine how many people might read it, or the emails some of them would send me, or the sometimes-mixed way I would feel about it only months after it came out. And I think it turned out well, or the way it needed to, or maybe both of those things. It told the story I needed to hear at the time I wrote it, which was: It's okay that you are a twenty-five-year-old woman who's never had a boyfriend. Or had sex. This doesn't mean there is something wrong with you, despite every cultural and social cue to the contrary.

I didn't start writing a book on purpose—I did it because a literary agent had read my writing on *The Hairpin* and asked if I'd thought about writing something longer. I hadn't, really, but I started anyway. Rylee helped me organize my life into a story, writing a list of former crushes and their defining characteristics on her whiteboard like a list of murder suspects. Her memory was often more precise than mine, so when I couldn't remember which exact party I'd been at when I'd kissed Ian, she would. Still, she had known me only since we were eighteen, living across the hall from each other in our freshman dorm, so before that, I was on my own. In a big, gray Rubbermaid bin stored in my parents' basement crawl space, thrown in among No Doubt's *Tragic Kingdom* and Hanson's *Middle of Nowhere* and other CDs I couldn't bring myself to throw away, I kept a handful of unfinished diaries from my childhood and teenage years. Paging through these helped me remember details I'd preferred to forget, like that I'd given my senior year crush my phone number in the form of a program in his graphing calculator.

I didn't know what my book was about when I started it, but seeing all my romantic failures lined up back-to-back, I realized there *was* something wrong with me. Or, not wrong with me, exactly, but different. As a teenager and then a college student I'd felt behind often enough, but not until I was twenty-four did I find myself entirely alone. It was at that point that I realized I no longer knew any woman my age who'd never dated anyone. I was deeply embarrassed by my lifelong singleness, so naturally, I decided to make it the subject of my book. On the off chance there was someone else like me out there, I wanted her to know she wasn't alone. I also wanted people to laugh at me the way I wanted them to laugh at me— not because of the mere fact of my virginal existence, but because of the way I described it. I hoped that in writing it all out I would come up with a conclusion or two so my book would feel satisfying, but I also wanted some answers for myself.

And as I wrote, I got them. By telling the story of every boy I'd ever liked, I developed a sense of agency and ownership over situations in which I'd felt helpless more often than not. Many of the boys I wrote about had been completely ambivalent to my existence. Our love affairs were prolonged, one-sided dirges. Rarely did they seem all that funny at the time, but writing about them, years after the fact, they became hilarious. More than that, they seemed . . . complete. With every boy I reexamined I was able to find a reason it wouldn't have worked out. He was only briefly between girlfriends, or he was a little stupid, or I wasn't all that into him after all. I did not omit my sadness or frustration, but I gave lots of credit to my hindsight. As I caught up to the present day, I was hoping to make a first boyfriend of a man in my graduate program. He seemed interested, and I excitedly wondered if I was about to derail my own story. But after we went out a couple of times, and he didn't kiss me, and I couldn't get myself to kiss him, he started dating somebody else. *Well,* I thought. It's better for the book anyway.

When I finished my book I believed every word I'd written. At the time I assumed that was the same thing as it being entirely and permanently true. When people balked at the idea of a memoir written by a twenty-five-year-old, I doubled down on every point I'd made. And I still don't think there is or should be a minimum age requirement for writing about one's life. Nor do I think anyone needs to have everything all figured out before they write about themselves. If that were the standard, there would be no memoirs at all. But I understand that paternalism a little better now, too. I understand the impulse of the slightly older person who wants to tell the slightly younger person she has no idea. I feel that way toward my earlier self.

If I didn't particularly want to get a boyfriend by the time I finished my book, I did think it would be great if things could work out so I could have one when my book came out, a year and a half later. That way it could be something I could serenely refer to in interviews. ("Are you in a relationship?" I envisioned being asked, and I would smile and demur, saying only that I was very happy.) That way, I could be the single girl who stayed single and was happy anyway, *and* the girl who did find love in the end. The book ended when I was twenty-five, and when it came out I'd be twenty-seven, and even though I didn't want my success measured in boyfriends, I didn't know how else I could prove that I had grown in those two years. I didn't want to feel like I had to prove anything, but I did. I couldn't get that weight off my shoulders.

The fall I moved to New York, a few months before my book came out, I'd had a six-month wind-up to a romance that petered out in one. When we'd finally kissed, I'd been disappointed by how little I felt. I hoped it would change, because I liked when he held my hand, and when he pulled me closer to him at bars. But after a few weeks he got even more annoyingly moody than usual, and I knew what that meant, so we made a date for him to dump me. I didn't cry when he did it—I was very impressed with myself and how composed I was when I walked away and left him there—but I know I cried a lot before and after. It seemed fundamentally unjust for him not to yank me around just a little bit longer, just long enough that I could call him my boyfriend first.

But then I got over it, because I started liking someone else. Though we saw each other at work every day, we communicated largely by Twitter and Gchat. He seemed mildly interested in me, which was refreshing after the empty effusiveness of his predecessor. Somehow I convinced myself his wishy-washiness was a kind of temperance—probably because he liked to talk about his principled hesitance toward dating a co-worker. (This became *very* funny later, when I heard he'd embarked upon a fourth or fifth office romance.) Some men are very good at encouraging the women they date to mistake their carelessness and callousness for shyness and awkwardness. And yet, all the ones I've known are invariably described by their male friends as very good guys. Whatever you say, man.

Anyway, this co-worker asked me out a couple of weeks before my book came out. We got dinner in Manhattan, and then met friends of his at a bar nearby. When the friends announced they were leaving for a bar in Brooklyn, I surprised myself by suggesting he and I go with, knowing that doing so meant I wouldn't be coming home that night. I was so sick of myself by then. I was mad at myself for not having had sex with the last guy when I'd had the chance, just because it hadn't felt all that great to make out with him drunk in the back of a cab. I was mad my book was about to come out, two years after I'd started it, and nothing demonstrable had changed since I'd finished it. I was tired of waiting for any of this to come naturally; I was twenty-seven years old. It was never going to feel natural. So I went home with him.

We didn't have sex. He didn't try, which I thought was *so sweet*. Besides, it was only our first date. After our second, I slept over again, and a few articles of clothing came off, but we didn't have sex then, either. Not really. But it was nice. He told me about places he wanted to take me that summer. It was February. I thought we were working up to it.

And then, a few days after that, my book came out.

It was the best day of my life thus far. All day at work I was on the Internet, tweeting at girls who were reading my excerpts and relating to what I'd written. My friends congratulated me and so did some strangers. My dad sent flowers to my office. That night I wore a beautiful dress to my book party, and while I listened to some of the writer friends I'd made read their own hilariously bad dating stories, I watched the door and waited for the guy I liked to get there. He was late, but he got there right before I started reading (I went last), and I told myself the important part was seeing me. And after I was done, he was nice to me, and stayed late at the after-party at a bar down the block.

I knew it was probably weird to be in his position,

dating the girl who, as a matter of public record, did not date. And when he abruptly canceled our third date, and then stopped texting me, and stopped looking at me, even, when we saw each other at work, I figured I'd been right. He'd known about the book before it came out, but I think the idea of a book about something is very different from the physical proof of one. Once it was an actual object existing out in the world, it wasn't hard to see myself in his eyes, and all guys' eyes, really, as a little bit desperate, and a little bit sad. I didn't feel that I was those things, or that my book as a whole came off that way, but there were these interviews and excerpts running online under headlines like "I Have Been Single for My Entire Life" and "Help Me, for I Am a Tragic, Old Virgin," and I imagine that's kind of hard to ignore. For me, at least, it was impossible.

Little by little, my pride and my gratitude for my book and its response were eroded by my growing anger at what I perceived to be its consequences. I was mad at men for a year—not just the one who'd hurt me most recently, but all of them. I was mad at myself, for having fulfilled my own prophecy. I had written a book about how weird and nervous and inexperienced I was with guys, and in doing so made all guys think I was too weird and nervous and inexperienced for them to date. "All guys" meant the last couple of assholes and maybe three other guys I interacted with that year, but I was convinced I had enough for a representative sample.

So, for a while, I hated my book. After a period of

feeling truly moved by the emails I received from young women who'd read it and related to what I'd written, I started feeling frustrated whenever a new message arrived in my inbox. I felt disconnected from the hopeful and happy person I'd been when I wrote that book, and I resented having to pretend to be her. Not that I really *had* to, nobody was making me, but when a nineteen-year-old stranger writes to you and asks how it is you stay positive and self-assured, you feel responsible for showing her that you still are.

It should have made me feel better to hear that my book had helped someone feel less alone. And for a long time, it did. But then somehow it started to make me feel even lonelier. Guilty, too—the book had come out, and already I was no longer the person I'd been when I wrote it. And not in a good way. Not in the way people clearly expected when they wrote me to ask what had happened in my life since the book ended. I didn't have the reassuring news they were hoping for. Instead of blossoming I had shriveled in on myself. I wasn't confident and independent and contentedly single. I was bitterly angry and I was exhausted. I hadn't learned a thing. I didn't want anything to do with men unless they could make me better. I wondered if getting a man to fuck me would make me better. I thought maybe I could enlist a friend, just get it over with. I even thought about how I'd word the text message. I didn't go through with it for the same reasons I don't go through with most things I've decided I won't do: pride, and fear. But I got close enough to feel certain I was not the person I'd written about. She had come undone.

6

SIGNIFICANT, OTHER

About six months after *Never Have I Ever* came out, I started seeing a therapist who was, at first, very validating of my frustration with men. Not just the ones who'd dumped me, but as a group, in general. She listened to my stories about the ones I'd briefly dated and was satisfyingly outraged on my behalf. She did not blame me for not wanting to date more of these people. And for a while, this was all I needed to hear. It was—is—normal to be a woman who finds it nearly impossible to muster the optimism necessary for dating men. It is normal to be angry that so many men are repeatedly enabled to treat women badly. It is normal to take stock of your smart and beautiful friends and then the dopey, dumbass, not-very-nice guys they're dating and think, *What the fuck?*

However.

It is also possible for some of that righteous fury to be informed by something else. And when I started to question more seriously if maybe that something else was playing a role here, I brought it up to my then-therapist. In a roundabout and stammery sort of way I asked her if she thought it seemed to her like, I don't know, maybe I was secretly . . . gay?

"I don't think that's what this is about," she said. "I think this is about your issues with men."

"Oh," I said. "Okay."

I was stunned. I wasn't a psychologist, but it seemed wrong for a therapist to so thoroughly dismiss something a patient brought up. I wasn't at all sure it was true, and I thought it probably wasn't. But still, why didn't she take it seriously?

Against my every instinct to trust credentialed authority figures over my own judgment, I canceled our next appointment and didn't make another one. I didn't know what my issue was; I just knew she wasn't going to be the one to help me find it.

For a long time I didn't have a crush on anybody at all. It was incredibly bleak. I haven't had all that many multi-month periods in my life in which I didn't have a crush on someone. Crushes are, sadly, one of the main ways I orient my otherwise bad memory; knowing it was Blake I liked in fifth grade and Colin in sixth helps me to remember who I was friends with, where my locker was, what my favorite outfit was that year.

When I did get a sort-of crush on someone, it was on someone several years younger who I only really knew from the Internet. But he was funny, and tall, and I was bored, so that was going to be enough. I went through all the usual symptoms: a twinge of pleasure each time he said something to me (or, like, favorited a tweet), a brief burst of ridiculous envy each time he appeared to flirt with a girl who wasn't me. I invited him to a party my roommate and I were having and was surprised when he actually showed up. While we shifted around into various group formations, he looked at me often enough that one of my friends pointed it out to me.

Eventually people started leaving, but he stayed: well past midnight, well after all our mutual friends had gone home and so had nearly everyone else, until the only people left in the kitchen were he and I. Even I could recognize what was going on. But as soon as I realized that sex was once again right in front of me, I knew I wasn't going to take it. And it wasn't about being afraid, or self-conscious, or wanting to move more slowly. I just didn't want to do it. I thought I was into him, but then it turned out I wasn't. After he'd gone home I lay awake in bed wondering if the same could be said for everyone else I'd ever wanted.

The idea of having sex with a woman first occurred to me as an option at the age of twenty-one. But that's all it ever was: an idea. It was just a fantasy—something I thought about only when I was alone, especially after watching *The L Word*—not anything I'd been moved to act on in real life. It wasn't like I was harboring secret sex feelings toward my friends. Like my friends, I had sex feelings toward Channing Tatum. Even if it was true that when I closed my eyes I sometimes pictured girls, when they were open, when I was scanning a room for people I might be attracted to, I was almost always looking at men. Until one day, I stopped.

The spring after I turned twenty-eight, one morning, on the subway to work, I realized my attraction to men was just . . . gone. I was looking all around me as usual, at the men seated across the car and hanging on railings above me and standing arms crossed against the doors, and I thought: *I don't want to sleep with any of you.*

I know a subway car full of people isn't all that many people. And it's not like it's all that unusual to get on a subway car and find not even one hot person in there with you. But this wasn't like that. There were at least four or five handsome enough men around me—nice-and-normal-looking guys who looked like guys my friends might date. My friends, but not me. It suddenly became clear that this wasn't about me being "picky." For the first time in my life, I chose to accept that I wasn't into most guys because I wasn't really all that into guys. And that was okay. I didn't *have* to like men. I don't know why that day, or why those men, but it was in that fifteen-minute subway ride that I realized, once and for all, that I wasn't straight. I didn't know what I was, but finally I knew what I wasn't.

Thank God, the next day I had therapy. I told my new therapist, whom I'd met a few months after dumping the previous one, about my subway-car epiphany. When she asked what I thought I might do differently now, I told her I'd switched my Tinder settings to show me women. "But I'm not sure whether it'll stay that way," I said. I knew that was okay, but hearing her tell me it was okay was important to me. She did. My therapist also asked how I felt about the idea of going on a date with a girl. "Nervous but intrigued," I said. "Like, nervous in a good way." Then she asked how I'd felt, in the past and now, at the idea of going on a date with a guy. "Nervous and pessimistic," I said. "Nervous in a bad way?" she said. I nodded. "So . . . dread?" she asked. "I think that's significant." I was like, *!!!*

All this time, almost all the way to thirty, I thought dating dread was normal. Everybody I know (and everyone I don't) complains about dating. It's supposed to suck. It's supposed to be agony. You're supposed to feel miserable on most of the first dates you go on, because most people are boring or bad for you. I asked my therapist: Doesn't everyone feel that way? "Not really," she said. Nervousness was normal; dread, though: that was different. Dread is for dentist appointments. Spring cleaning. Family reunions, if you can't or don't drink. Things you do not want to do but must do anyway.

Over the next half hour my therapist ran me through a series of these side-by-side comparisons. Did I worry about running out of things to talk about on a date with a girl? (No.) What about with a guy? (Yes.) Given the choice between hanging out with my female friends and going out to a bar to meet guys, which would I pick?

(Friends, always.) How did I feel when I pictured myself in bed with a man? (Like the Discovery show, naked and afraid.) And with a woman? (Let's just say I could picture it pretty easily.) After each of my responses, my therapist would say, "I think that's significant!!" Eventually the word "significant" started seeming like some sort of therapist's code word for "kinda gay," which I found hilarious. This was one of those groundbreaking therapy sessions that you realize will mark a turning point in your life even while you're still in it. Everything was funny. And significant. I was giddy and full of hope.

I came out in waves and in two different directions. Not counting the handful of times I'd run the gay hypothesis by Rylee before retracting it a week later, the first two people I told were work friends with whom I shared a three-person chat room ostensibly devoted to our thoughts and feelings concerning One Direction. I eased into things by telling them about my recently M.I.A. attraction to men. Then I mentioned, as casually as possible, that I'd been wondering if I should try dating women. They asked me a few diagnostic questions—Had I thought about this before? Had I done anything about it yet?—and that was it. I was out to someone, as something, and that was enough pressure let off my chest for the moment. I didn't plan to tell anyone else until there was something more concrete and specific to tell, and I had no idea when that would be.

A couple of weeks (and therapy sessions) later, I had

switched my Tinder over to show me only girls. One woman I matched with asked for my phone number right off the bat, and we sent each other strings of slightly baffled texts as we tried to figure out each other's sense of humor. I didn't know her last name, so I gave her one: "Tinder." I was not interested in everyone I talked to, but I was happy to talk to everyone at least once. It was painless and undramatic and nothing like my previous experiences on Tinder talking to men. I felt proud, and capable, and I told my work friends all about it, thrilled by how thrilled they were for me. It felt so good to talk about my dating life outside the framework of my own sadness and my friends' gentle pity. I wanted more. So I decided I would come out to Chiara.

The first time I tried to tell her, we were at a bagel shop in Park Slope, near her new apartment, catching up before work. I kept my eyes down, watching myself smear excess cream cheese off my bagel onto the brown tissue paper it came in, and tried to segue the conversation over to lesbianism using the only entry point I could think of: Ruby Rose.

"Did you watch the new *Orange Is the New Black* season yet?" I asked Chiara.

"Yep."

"What did you think of Ruby Rose?"

Chiara shrugged. "She wasn't *great*."

"No," I agreed.

This isn't going to work, I thought.

The next time I tried to come out to Chiara, a few days later, she Gchatted me to tell me she was engaged. "I really, really wanted to tell you the other day, when we got a bagel," she wrote, "but I hadn't even told my parents yet."

"I decided I'd tell you if you commented on the ring," she added.

"You were wearing one????" I couldn't believe that I, a person who notices when the guy at the deli trims his beard, could have missed an engagement ring on one of my best friends' hands while sitting next to her. Evidently I was preoccupied. So I congratulated her, and demanded she send me a picture of the ring, and asked her to tell me the story of how her then-fiancé asked her. And I decided I would wait a little bit longer to tell her, not wanting to steal Chiara's thunder by coming out.

I gave it eight days, and then I Gchatted her to tell her I'd been "talking to" girls on Tinder. I was shaking as I typed. I was more afraid to tell her than I was to tell my parents, and felt the need to do so more urgently. For as long as I had known her, Chiara had been a sort of dating mentor to me. Even before she met her husband, even when she was as single as I was, I treated her like an expert, and she acted accordingly. In giving me advice, my other friends were reassuring and validating, but Chiara could be brutal. "What am I doing wrong?" is usually meant as a rhetorical question, but Chiara always had a list ready. Sometimes I resented her for it, but I was the one who kept asking. I have spent a lot of time in therapy trying to figure out what kind of power it is that I've given her. Mainly, I think, she is a know-it-all, and I love that in a friend. During the three or so years I knew her before I knew I was gay, I had ached for answers. I spent those three years asking all the wrong questions, but Chiara answered them as best she could. And now, knowing that she'd been "wrong"—insofar as the answer to my singleness had not, in fact, been about how little I smiled at men, or how many dates I went on with them, or all the many other practical things she had suggested, believing me to be as straight as I said—I felt almost sorry. Like I was abandoning this project she'd worked so hard on. Like maybe she would think I was trying to cheat the system.

Immediately, Chiara wrote back: "Oh! Yeah?"

I told her that her reaction was a little underwhelming, given the way my heart was flying out of my chest. "You have to react delicately!!!!" she wrote. (Even in this unprecedented situation, she had such a clear idea as to what was proper.) Then she asked me some questions: what brought this about, and when it started. And when I told her I'd been trying to tell her for two weeks, she wrote "but I told you about my engagement!!!!" and we both typed a lot of laughter in the way that indicates it is actually happening in real life. She told me that if we *were* together in real life, she would give me a big hug. We talked a little bit about the timeline and the questions I still had and the things my therapist had said, and together did a little retroactive putting-together of two and two. Because even though I knew enough to know that this had become something I needed to share (and thus make real), I still didn't know as much as I wanted, which was: everything.

"It's just confusing because I'm not . . . in love with my friends!" I wrote.

"Right," Chiara wrote back, "but"—and here I got

antsy and excited, like I always did when I could tell she
was about to make some confident assertion—

> you don't LIKE guys. You don't like THINGS about them
> that like
> i think people who are attracted to men sexually DO kind of like
> or like
> I dunno
> well, no, i honestly don't know.

Frankly, this stunned me. Freely admitted uncertainty
was not what I signed up for when I first tried to get Chiara to be friends with me. For along with the criticism she
gave me came a great deal of insight as to things I could
not or did not want to see. She is perhaps the most annoyingly perceptive human being that I have ever met, which
is part of what makes her such an incredible writer, and
why I find it nearly impossible to discount her opinion on
pretty much anything. And yet, even she had not known
all there was to know about me. It was a massively reliev-
ing thing to realize, and a little sad, too.

Having waited long enough to come out to Chiara, I
came out to almost everyone else as quickly as I possibly
could. I texted Rylee, whom I'd justified not telling first
because I had told her *most*; I emailed my two younger
brothers on one thread, asking them to rate their level of
surprise between one (not surprised) and ten (flabber-
gasted). One of them said four and the other said two, and
if I hadn't been so moved and so grateful, I would have
found their brotherly nonchalance slightly irritating. But
I also asked my brothers not to mention my email to my

parents yet. Nothing about my parents' politics or person-
alities led me to believe they would be unhappy or unsup-
portive, but that didn't mean I wouldn't be desperately
uncomfortable. My family are ex-Catholic Midwesterners
who started allowing their kids a glass of wine at Thanksgiving dinner only a few years ago and who don't talk
about sex. I would prefer for my father, especially, to forever think of me as a sort of sexless android. Even still, if
I was going to have this conversation with them, I wanted
it to be in person, so I could see their faces and they could
see mine. I wanted to be able to be hugged afterward. But
I also wanted to wait until I had a set of concrete facts I
could deliver: a specific person with a name, rather than
the hypothetical possibility of an entire sex. I had every
hope that I would one day meet this specific person, but I
had no idea when.

I never expected it would be so soon.

7

OKCUPID, REDUX

Two or three times before I officially came out even to myself, I switched my Tinder over to show me women. At first I set it up to show me both men and women, but I soon realized that this was more or less the same as having it show me only men, because there are way, way more straight men on Tinder than queer women. I would have to swipe through, like, fifty guys to see even one girl. And because the whole reason I'd made the switch in the first place was that I was still trying to evaluate whether I was actually interested in women or merely wished that I was, it was women I wanted to focus on. So I made my Tinder gay. That first time, I didn't really want to match with anyone—I just wanted to see the girls that were on there, and to see how it felt to be there as someone looking for women. It was an experiment. I swiped left on women for ten or fifteen minutes, relieved not to feel anything more toward them than I did the men I passed over the same way. But then a profile came up which made me pause. It belonged to a girl around my age, wearing a leather jacket and a beanie over shoulder-length brown hair. She was pretty, slightly tomboyish but femme-ier than any girl I'd been attracted to in the past, so much so that I was not sure whether I was attracted to her or wanted to look like her. My thumb started to hurt, and I realized it remained against the screen, suspending her in Tinder purgatory. And that's where she stayed for two days. Instead of choosing one way or the other, I simply closed out of Tinder altogether. Because even though I wasn't sure exactly what I thought of her, I didn't want to reject her. Her bio was brief, but funny, and her pictures made her seem interesting and fun. She did not fit the extremely narrow idea I had then about what a queer girl looks like—which is to say, more boyish, or more androgynous—and that, more than anything, made it hard to look away.

Eventually, after I wore myself out trying to decide why exactly I was fixated on this girl and what that meant, I swiped right on her, and we matched. I was both flattered and panicked; I'd been so singularly focused on how I should proceed that it had not really occurred to me to wonder what she would do, or had already done. I did not have very long to wonder what would happen next; my phone vibrated with a new message while it was still in my hand.

It said: "Are you the same Katie whose articles I've read online?"

Well, fuck, I thought. She recognized me. And if she'd read things I'd written, she was probably wondering what I was doing looking for girls on a dating app. She had probably taken a screenshot of my profile and maybe even texted it to one or more of her friends. I am not proud to admit this is where my brain went, but I began to envision a scenario in which my sexuality (and by extension, my character) was called into question by any number of serious young book bloggers. My first book would be recalled for factual inaccuracies, and then I would have to go on an apology tour for a $20,000 speaker's fee. And I wasn't ready for all that. I didn't have an explanation for myself, let alone anyone else. I did not want to take apart the person I'd spent twenty-eight years becoming only to find that I couldn't make anything solid from what was left. I felt that if I replied to that girl and told her that I was the person she was thinking of, it would only lead to more questions. I didn't want more questions. So I did not reply. I deleted Tinder. And almost a year's worth of confusion and anxiety later, I downloaded OkCupid in its place.

This is not meant to be some kind of dating-app endorsement. Both of these apps have value. It's just about knowing your audience and your intentions. For me, Tinder was an excuse. Tinder was what I used when I wanted to reassure the bossier of my friends that I was doing my dating due diligence. Tinder, for me, is pure performance. I swiped left on, like, everybody. I didn't have enough information to work with, and I wasn't putting myself out there in any meaningful way. I knew that I needed more than five photos and a one-line biography to work from. I also knew I was far too terrified to participate in low-

stakes, first-date casual sex just yet. Tinder isn't just a
hookup app, but, at least where I live, among my age
group, it has more of a casual-sex bent to it than OkCupid
does. Plus, there just weren't all that many girls on there.
I would swipe through five or eight of them and then the
app would tell me there was no one left, at least until tomorrow. And this was in New York City.

At work I complained about my bad luck to my friend
Mackenzie, and she said a lesbian friend of hers said that
all the gay girls were on OkCupid. "Ughhhhhhhh," I said.
"Fine."

It was with great trepidation and a little excitement
that I created a brand-new OkCupid profile. I uploaded
my photos and described myself as charmingly as possible. I filled out my stats—5'11", agnostic, not much drinking and even fewer drugs, a Sagittarius, not that I believe
in all that. Then it came time to label my orientation, and
I froze up. It was all well and good for my therapist to tell
me it was okay not to know exactly what to call myself,
but I had to enter something. It's getting more acceptable
and cooler these days to say "no labels" or that "labels
don't matter," but when it comes to filling out forms, it
sure helps to have a word handy. I had set my profile to
show me only women, but that didn't mean I was ready to
use "gay" or "lesbian" to describe myself. I wasn't sure it
was fair, and I wasn't out to my family or most of my
friends, let alone the public. I remembered that girl who
recognized me on Tinder, and I picked "bisexual," in no
small part because I was paranoid the same thing would
happen again.

It didn't take long for me to realize that the number-one thing I'd always hated about OkCupid with men didn't apply to OkCupid with women. I have since talked to women who've gotten their fair share of sexually aggressive messages from other women, but in my short time there, I did not receive a single gross or insulting message. (Full disclosure: I was on there for only about two weeks. But still. Spend a week on OkCupid looking for men and you'll get enough garbage for a lifetime.) It was all, Hi, how are you, my name is Whatever, you seem cool. Or hi, you're cute, I love *The X-Files*, too.

Each time I matched with a girl I'd "winked" at or whatever, I got heart palpitations. Then I'd talk to her, and usually our conversation would trail off after a few messages. For the first time in my life I did not feel racked with guilt if I didn't want to respond to someone. Nor did I feel ruined if she did not respond to me. That was just what dating was; sometimes two people like each other and sometimes it doesn't line up. People had been trying to tell me this for years, but it had always felt so much heavier than that. It had felt like endless failure. But talking to girls was different. I loved talking to girls. I'd been doing it my entire life. And if there was still something in me that felt like I was playing a character—Girl Who Effortlessly Flirts with Other Girls—there was a larger part that wondered if it was supposed to have been this painless all along.

Four days into my time on gay-girl OkCupid, I had two dates lined up one night after another. I know there are people out there who do this all the time, but for me, whose M.O. with online dating was to meet approximately one man, one time, once a year, this was, well . . .

significant. I felt nervous, *very* nervous, but excited, too. Both girls were cute, and seemed normal. I was interested in one more than the other, which made me feel like a genuine casual dater. Someone with a roster of possibilities. Finally I understood why my friends had always told me to just "go on a bunch of dates"—it spread out the pressure. When you go on only one date a year, it is pretty easy to let it mean too much. Making two dates in the same week was deeply out of character for me, but then, the whole point of all this was to try out for another role.

My first date was on a Monday night with a girl named Lydia, and all day long all I wanted to do was throw up. It wasn't the same kind of nausea I'd felt before a date with a guy—the kind I hoped would transform into a bona fide illness so I could cancel with a guilt-free conscience. I wanted to feel perfect—I just didn't. I could barely eat, and that never happens to me. I couldn't focus on work. I am pretty sure that all I did that day was get up from my desk to refill my water glass or to sit in the bathroom for as long as I felt I could get away with it without people thinking I was having some kind of gastrointestinal problem. Toward the end of the day I walked over to our office manager's desk and quietly asked for some Pepto-Bismol. When she held out the box I took four.

I got to the bar ten minutes early, like I always do when attempting to get somewhere exactly on time. Sitting under an umbrella on the bar's garden patio, looking at the straight couples on dates all around me, I wondered what people would think when they saw me sitting with another girl. Would they buy it? Was I passing? Would it be obvious that I had never done this before? How does a

Never before in my life had I made anything resembling "the first move." I was always too nervous, I thought, and too afraid of being rejected. But that night, I realized that wasn't quite it. I was nervous to text Lydia, and also afraid of being rejected, but my desire to talk to her again, as soon as possible, outweighed those fears. So while I stood in my kitchen shoving graham crackers into my face, because we hadn't eaten dinner and I was starving and a little dizzy, I talked to Chiara about what I should say. She suggested I say what she'd texted Mark (the man she'd eventually marry) after their first date: "Mark! I think you're great. Thanks for the fun night." It's simple and direct, she explained. It says you're interested in them without having to explicitly say you want to see them again. I knew she was right, so I texted Lydia, slowly and carefully: "Lydia! I think you're great. Thanks for the fun night." Then I waited a truly agonizing six minutes, during which time Chiara repeatedly talked me off the ledge. And then Lydia wrote back and asked if I'd want to hang out again. I was so happy all I sent in return was "DUH."

I liked Lydia so much I canceled the other date I'd scheduled for the next day, a Tuesday, and instead made a second one with her for the following Saturday night. In the meantime, we texted constantly, and I worried she would Google me. Our first date had lasted four hours, but I had not told her in that time that I hadn't dated women before. I'd told her I'd written a book, but didn't say much about its topic. I didn't want to scare her, and historically, the book had scared people away. Or I had spent a long time thinking it had. In any case, it was a first date, and I don't think anyone owes anyone much on a first date—it's a very preliminary vetting. I figured that I would talk about it if and when it became more relevant, which would probably happen as soon as I really liked someone. I just didn't expect to really like someone so soon.

On Saturday, Lydia and I met at the subway stop between our apartments and got on the Q to Coney Island. I'd bought us two tickets to a Brooklyn Cyclones game, realizing only after we got there that they were for "*Star Wars* Night." At first we were under the impression that all this meant was that people had come to the game wearing *Star Wars* hats and T-shirts, and you could buy a promotional *Star Wars* soda cup for eight dollars. But then, after the first inning, a number of people dressed in *Star Wars* costumes ran onto the field and began acting out a plotline involving Darth Vader kidnapping Princess Leia and hiding her somewhere inside MCU Park. As the actors mouthed their lines, their prerecorded voices played over the speakers. This provided a great source of small talk for Lydia and me, which was helpful because it was soon apparent that we were both considerably more nervous than we'd been when we first met. We bought two ciders, a Diet Coke, a burger, and a soft pretzel between us, and we barely touched any of it. In every moment I wasn't talking, I was thinking about how to tell her who I really was.

Soon enough, she gave me my cue. "I want to hear more about this book," she said. So I told her all about it, and watched her face, waiting for her to check out. But she didn't. Instead she asked if I had gone out with another girl before, and after a record-breaking-long "um," I said no, I hadn't. Barely ten days earlier I had come out to Chiara as a woman who, after a lifetime spent trying to date guys, wanted to date women instead. And here I was on one such gay date, coming out as a former straight girl. I felt like apologizing and laughing and throwing up. Somehow I kept all three in. Then Lydia said, "But you still date guys, too, right?" And though I had labeled myself "bisexual" on OkCupid, not wanting to lie, not knowing how else to reconcile my past with my future, though I had spent years trying to nail down the exact breakdown of my attractions, I didn't hesitate or hedge. I knew. "No," I said. "I don't."

The baseball game ended (the Cyclones won), and a group of thirty actors rushed the field, beginning a mass, make-believe lightsaber fight that lasted nearly twenty minutes. When they were done, fireworks exploded over the park to the tune of, appropriately enough, Katy Perry's "Firework." Already it had been a perfect date, and it wasn't even over.

As we walked away from the park, Lydia took my hand, and when I looked at her she said, "Just remember, I'm nervous, too." We walked to Luna Park and bought tickets for a haunted-house-themed ride called the Ghost Hole, a complete waste of money, unless you want an excuse to sit very close to someone in the dark. We walked the boardwalk until we found an empty bench to sit on. Then she kissed me, and I felt the thing I was supposed to have felt when I kissed guys. A few minutes later, someone yelled, "Get a room!"

There was so much about the circumstances of our meeting that seemed crazy to me. I couldn't believe she lived only one and a half blocks away from me, and worked in a shop across the street from me, and I had never seen her. I couldn't believe that I'd had such a great first date (and second, and third . . .) with the first woman I'd gone out with. Or that I'd met her on the very dating website I'd spent so much time hating and avoiding. I couldn't believe we were still together, and happy. I couldn't believe how natural it all felt. All those times I'd opened a dating app hoping to find love with the very first person I met, and look—it actually kind of happened.

I told my parents about Lydia after we'd been dating for about two weeks, but not, initially, by choice. The plan had been to tell them the next time I was in Minnesota, at the end of August. But early one morning in late July, my mom texted me to tell me about a dream she'd had in which I brought home a man I'd fallen in love with. (Apparently his name was James.) Just to be clear: this isn't something that happens with us. We don't text all that much, and when we do, it tends to be something about something my parents watched on MSNBC, or a picture of their Australian shepherd, Kiah, or a brag about their snowfall. Nor has my mother ever been the type of mother who asks when I'll finally bring a boyfriend home. She did not drop hints. This text was different, and eerie. I knew right then that I couldn't wait any longer to tell her. So I called her, still lying in bed, and I told her I *had* met someone recently, actually. But she was a woman. Her name was Lydia. I felt relieved the way I feel relieved when I've gotten onto an airplane and the flight attendants have closed the door and I can't get out of it even if I really, really want to.

My mom responded to my news with a perfectly Minnesotan "Oh!" She asked all the questions she would've had I been telling her I'd met a man—age, job, how we met—and some she wouldn't have: Did it feel normal when I kissed her? (Yes.) Was I nervous about holding her hand in public? (Not often, but sometimes.) She told me she was happy if I was happy, and that she would love me no matter what. Then she told me I should call my dad separately, but not for a couple of hours, because they were headed to Byerlys for groceries. Both she and my dad would tell me that day that my being gay may take some getting used to, but I said that was okay. It would for me, too.

Girl #3

· ·

Maya, seventh grade. Maya was popular but also un-interested, which everyone knows is cooler than caring. She looked like an Abercrombie model, blue eyes and pouty lips, and when she wore overalls over a tank top and her hair in pigtails it looked so much different than when I did. She was best friends with another popular girl, and somehow, together, they decided I was funny. Another big plus for me was that unlike theirs, my homework was always done. Maya and I were in World History together, and when it came time to do the widely dreaded concept-map project, we chose each other as partners. She came over to my house after school a few afternoons to work on it, and on the floor of my bedroom she watched me put it together almost entirely by myself. I did not care at all.

8

GOLD STAR

Here are some of the things I worried about whenever I considered having sex with a man: How it was going to fit. Whether or not to say I hadn't done it before. What he would say if I did. How much it was going to hurt. Bleeding. Ruined sheets. That thing that someone told me once about how they always put down a towel first—was I supposed to do that? What was I supposed to do with my face. What if he kept the lights on. What would he think of my body. Was I going to have to strip naked outside the bed like in a movie, because I just don't know if I have the gravitas. Was I supposed to talk during, and if so, what was I going to say. What was I supposed to do with the balls. (Did I *have* to do something with the balls, or could I treat them as garnish?)

What if his back was super hairy and I yelped in surprise. What if I wasn't doing whatever the right thing is to be doing with one's pubic hair these days. What if he made weird noises during. What if I did. Maybe that's what music is for, but when was I supposed to put it on so that it wasn't weird. Oh my god: what kind of music. Do people prepare playlists in advance. What if, when it was over, I thought it went well, but he thought I was a dead fish. How did I become something better than a fish.

What I worried about when preparing to have sex with a woman: I don't remember. I know I was nervous. I know I was concerned I wouldn't know what to do right away. (I hate not being amazing at everything I do the first time I do it.) But that was pretty much it. I wanted her more than I wanted to avoid feeling embarrassed or inept. For the first time in my life, my nervousness wasn't enough to hold me back.

I was twenty-four before I ever learned proper heterosexual handjob technique, and even then it was only on my best friend's forearm.

I'll give myself a little credit and say that I probably would have figured it out eventually. I'm no expert, but it is my understanding that there are only so many ways to go wrong with a hand and a penis. Presumably the person attached to the penis will let you know if you're doing something insane, like playing air flute on it. Besides, I'd read *Cosmopolitan*. I had the general idea, but I was very concerned about the specifics.

The impetus for this tutoring session was an unspecified hang-out-but-maybe-date with a boy I liked from grad school. First we were people who stared at each other across the Organizational Management classroom, and then we were friends, and then one weekend I told him to tell me if there were "any parties going on," and, much to my surprise, he did. We went to one such party together, drank beer and stood too close to each other. Then he walked me home, and when we paused outside my apartment's front door, I promptly leapt onto the stairs to escape kissing range. I wanted to have kissed him, but instinctively, I wanted to avoid the actual doing of it. Once inside my door I felt a familiar disappointment with myself, a deep disgust with my passivity, my fear, my reflexive chasteness. I vowed that the next whatever-it-was would be different, and so, that weekend, I started to prepare for the thing I had, for years, told disbelieving nurse practitioners I had nothing to do with: sexual activity.

In order to feel like I was making progress, I knew I'd have to do more with this guy than just make out. Making out was old news. I'd already done it with, like, seven whole guys. Maybe drunken dance-floor kissing was enough to make me feel accomplished and included when I was still in college, but I was twenty-four now, and it was starting to hit me that I was officially the oldest person I knew who'd never made it even halfway to second base. I wasn't especially sorry I hadn't had sex with any of my previous options, but I felt that if I didn't have sex with this guy, it would be a bigger failure than it would have been when I was just twenty-two.

Still, I didn't want to get too far ahead of myself. There was some before-sex sex stuff I would be cool with

doing on a second date, probably. *No big deal,* I panicked.
All I had to do was consult the best sexpert I knew: Rylee.
Her qualifications? Having had sex with more than three
people. And, more important, a patient, uncondescending
attitude toward both my incredibly specific questions and
my mildly horrified reaction to the answers.

In college my friends and I had developed a preference
for each other's beds over our own, playing Goldilocks
around the dormitory floor (and later, our off-campus
house). The just-right bed was chosen depending on the
issue at hand. On Colleen's bed we recounted drunken
embarrassments from the night before. On mine we eval-
uated one another's going-out outfits. On Rylee's—so
long as her very Catholic roommate was out—we talked
about sex. And unless we were asleep or away, our doors
were always open to one another. So it happened that I
crossed the living room between our rooms and climbed
onto Rylee's bed, interrupting her regression-analysis
homework to ask for a crash course in handjob delivery.
She reacted as calmly as if I'd asked her to explain serial
correlation to me, again.

"Okay," she said, putting down her pen. "Couple
things."

First she demonstrated on her own arm. I watched
with my chin in my palm as she clamped her right hand
tightly—surprisingly tightly, I thought—around her left
forearm and tugged it up and down. "See how the skin's
moving but my hand isn't sliding?"

I made a noise indicating lukewarm agreement.

"Same thing with a penis," she said.

"Hm."

She held out her forearm. As though it were a snake I was trying not to spook, I wrapped my right hand around it as slowly as possible, leaving a quarter inch of space between her skin and mine.

"Tighter," she said.

"I feel like I'm going to hurt it."

"I mean, don't squeeze, just grip." I gripped. "Okay, now . . . go." I immediately loosened my grip and slid my hand up and down her arm.

"No, no," she said, laughing. "Do you think that's going to do anything?"

If I knew that, I thought, *I wouldn't be in this position.* Rylee closed her hand over mine, tightening it around her arm, and then moved it up and down for me, showing me how the skin on her wrist creased up as my fist moved toward it. I know that all of this sounds incredibly sexual, but trust me when I say that it was the least sexual sex workshop that has ever taken place. This did not feel like information I could actually put into practice. It felt like being shown how to change your car's oil, and realizing halfway through the demonstration that you would sooner pay someone else to do it than ever have to do it yourself.

What I didn't quite put together then was that I wanted to know how to give a handjob and a blowjob not because I actually wanted to give guys handjobs and blowjobs but because I knew that they were components of having sex with men, and I wanted to have had sex with at least one man. There was no part of me that was excited by the idea of giving a guy I liked a blowjob. For one thing, my dentist is always telling me what a small mouth

I have. Logistically, I just wasn't sure how it was going to work. For another, there was the spit-versus-swallow question, which, according to TV shows, implied some sort of value judgment I wasn't sure how to make. Whenever Rylee and I talked about blowjobs I spent half the time wincing. I'd tell her I didn't think that sounded like something I wanted to do, and she said she didn't blame me; it wasn't exactly her favorite thing in the world, either.

Because I was not a Christian saving myself for marriage, or otherwise determined to remain a virgin until a specific point in time, I had long considered my sexlessness accidental. It wasn't part of my platform. Sex just didn't happen to me. That's largely how I thought of it: a phenomenon that existed almost entirely outside myself—something that seemed much less scary, and much more within reach, to almost everyone I knew. What little responsibility I took was in acknowledging that there were times I probably could have had sex with someone and neglected to take the steps necessary to find out. Let's say a mousetrap had consciousness, and it lay down somewhere very few mice like to go—maybe the middle of a very busy sidewalk. Then let's say that on the rare occasion a mouse did come close enough, instead of snapping its silver arm down across its back, the mousetrap was like, *Ehhh, I'll get the next one.* Then the mousetrap would feel very bad for itself for a while. It was kind of like that.

My mother has always told me I have to say no to something several times before I'll say yes to it, and though I do not think she'd love to hear that rule applied to sex, it fits there, too. Even at twenty-seven, and by then thoroughly fed up with myself, I was still hesitating. That year I had more clear, unobscured, inarguable opportunities to have sex than I'd ever had, and I'd rejected every one. I had my reasons—he was too drunk; I had a thing early the next morning; I was waiting for the third date—but at the root of it, very deep down, there was a growing suspicion I didn't know what to do with: that perhaps I had not had sex with these men simply because I did not want to. And if I did not want to have sex with men I had allegedly liked for months before I got in their beds, I did not know what men I *would* want to have sex with.

Toward the end of what turned out to be our truly perfect second date, Lydia asked if I'd slept with a girl before, and I said no. I'd already told her I hadn't been out with a girl before, so I was a little annoyed that she kept making me state my inexperience in different ways, but I was too high on adrenaline to do anything else but continue confessing. We'd been making out on a boardwalk bench in that urgent sort of way that forces the issue of sex. Which was a way I'd never really made out with anyone before. I was sitting slumped far enough down into my seat so that she, five inches shorter, could put her arm around my shoulder and I could rest my head on hers. While I answered her questions, I was looking at the ocean instead of her. But each time she was like, "Oh, okay!" And when I did look at her, I could tell it really wasn't a big deal. She was unfazed, if a little surprised. Maybe it's that queer people are more familiar with atypical timelines, and being someone's first. Maybe this woman was special.

After a couple more very good dates and a lot more excellent making out, we picked an upcoming night to be the first time she "slept over"—a not-very-euphemistic euphemism for the first time we'd, you know. Do it.

That night my roommate and I were having a party, and it was still well under way when Lydia and I—both of us a bit drunk, tired, antsy, having known all day what would eventually happen—decided we'd had enough waiting. We retreated into my room, at the opposite end of the apartment from the remaining partiers, and closed the door. And locked it. Or so I thought.

When someone opened my bedroom door five or ten minutes later, it was, visually speaking, the worst possible time. I do not know why someone opened my door, apart from alcohol-induced confusion, or a mistaken belief that this was where they'd left their coat. Nor do I know who it was, because my eyes were closed, and I hope to die without finding out. No sooner had we heard the creak of the door opening than Lydia's foot shot backward, slamming it closed. She played Division I soccer in college and has the reflexes to prove it.

"Oh my god," I said.

"Who was that?"

"I don't know! Do you think they saw?"

"I don't know," said Lydia, in a way that clearly meant *yes, probably.*

Maybe our unintentional pervert was looking over his or her shoulder when they twisted the knob and pressed the door open. Maybe, thanks to Lydia's athleticism, they didn't see anything. But probably they did. And while that was embarrassing, and imperfect, and so different from the way I'd imagined it in my head, it was also comfortable, and natural, and nice. It was good enough to know it was right. And I knew, I could already tell, that it was only going to get better.

favorite Hanson brother (Taylor). *NSYNC was fine. The
Backstreet Boys were fine. 98 Degrees was hilarious. I
owned most of these albums, and liked them well enough,
but my interest ended when I turned my Discman off. I
didn't have T-shirts or posters. I didn't collect magazine
cutouts and tape them to my walls. I never went to any of
their concerts. I didn't know, like, *trivia*. I knew which
band member I believed to be the Cute One in each case,
but even then it was more a necessary rite of passage than
a passion. For a time I considered myself a JC Chasez girl,
and finding others who felt the same way provided me
with, if not actual friends, a few moments of pleasant
small talk. But I did not care about any of these bands as
entities. I did not suffer when they broke up.

If every woman is born with a reserve of manic fangirl
enthusiasm, mine survived my adolescence untapped.

And then, One Direction.

I was aware of the band before I went crazy for them,
but only as a group of teenagers who sang that song about
how hot girls don't need to wear makeup because they are
already hot. Then two years went by, and the band released their second album, and something amazing happened right around that same time: they grew up. For
someone my age, it would have been a little bit inappro-
priate to fawn over One Direction in their first couple of
years; they were teenagers, and obvious ones. One of them
(Niall—the Irish one) had braces. Then they grew up just
enough to stop plastering their hair across their foreheads.
Most of them were at least twenty by 2013, except for
Harry, who I learned was nineteen years old. Having just

seen the video for "Best Song Ever" for the first time, I decided I didn't care. He was the most beautiful boy I had ever seen in my life.

A few months later, when our friend from work, Matt, mentioned he had two extra tickets to the One Direction show at MetLife Stadium that summer, my friend Arianna and I decided to go. At that time we were low-level fans only. I'd downloaded only their two newest singles, and while I thought that Harry Styles was very cute, I was satisfied by seeing a handful of red-carpet photos of him and the others every couple of months. The main reason we decided to pay $125 to go to New Jersey to see a preteen's band was because we thought it would be funny. And it was. Matt designed us matching T-shirts to wear, a collage of Harry's faces in the shape of a heart with the message "Harry Styles Come to BuzzFeed" underneath. We found our seats, way up high, and looked all around at the sea of girls, most of them under the age of fifteen, and their parents. We decided to get beers and there was no line at all, anywhere, because so few people there were over twenty-one. Before the show started the speakers blasted a playlist clearly meant to be retro and hip, and all of it was the music that was cool when I was thirteen.

When the band came onstage, we screamed. Arianna and I didn't know most of the songs, but we sang along to those we did. I took dozens of terrible, blurry photos, and just one or two in which Harry's face was clearly visible from the big-screen projection at the back of the stage. This was during his head-wrap phase: he was just then starting to grow out his hair. It is probably not a coinci-

dence that my love for One Direction grew in direct proportion to the length of Harry Styles's hair. When I left
that first show I was entertained but not yet a full-on fangirl. That came a few months later, in September, when
the boys—that's what I started calling them, "the boys," a
telltale sign that one has crossed over—released the first
single off their new album ("Steal My Girl"). Soon after
that, they released the video, in which Harry Styles wears
a leopard-print trench coat, his shoulder-length hair flow-
ing in the wind. From then on I was a goner. Harry Styles
was the only man that mattered.

I became friends with other die-hard 1D fans somewhat automatically. We were drawn to one another like
starry-eyed magnets. These were the girls in my office who
huddled around the newsroom TVs when the boys appeared on a morning talk show, who tweeted heart-eyes
emojis alongside pictures of Zayn's hair curl at the 2014
AMAs, who instant-messaged one another photos of their
every red-carpet appearance and photo spread. Three
months after we first saw them in concert, a group of us
bought tickets for their next New York/New Jersey show,
eleven months in advance.

At the height of my 1D mania, my equally obsessed
friend Mackenzie and I texted back and forth about them
almost hourly. For a month that winter I was on book
leave from work, staying at my parents' house in Minnesota. In the mornings I wrote and edited my manuscript
from the armchair in the living room, and every afternoon, all afternoon, I read books and texted about Harry
Styles. We debated the merits of the feathered-hat phase

and then the heeled-boots one; we kept a ranking of our favorite-ever Harry looks. We examined paparazzi photos of him with rumored girlfriends, and dissected Tumblr fan theories about him and Taylor Swift. Never in my life have I been so obsessed with a celebrity, or anyone for that matter. No level of trivia was irrelevant, no number of slightly different photos from the same event was too many. Everything that was available, I had to consume. I watched the band's documentary, *This Is Us,* twice, and I finally sympathized with the kind of girl who could be seen sobbing, reaching, trying to attach herself to the tour bus in hopes that she will be plucked from the crowd, carried away to be both fan-in-residence and Harry Styles's wife.

There were a few times that year when Harry Styles came to New York City. That's how I learned that being a superfan of a celebrity is a very different story when you live in a major city. When I lived in Minnesota I felt equal proximity to every celebrity, which is to say, about the distance from me to the moon. Generally speaking Minnesota is not a place that celebrities who are not from Minnesota ever come to. I never knew what it was like to come across pictures of one at a restaurant or shop and go, "Oh my god, I was just there!" But celebrities are in New York all the time. A whole bunch of them live here. It is absurd to me that I live in the same city as Taylor Swift, and I don't even have strong feelings about Taylor Swift. When I see a celebrity (and honestly it can be anyone) I invariably freeze up like an iguana trying to blend into its background. I don't want to be witnessed seeing a celebrity, because I am positive that any celebrity who did see me looking would be able to tell that I am not cool, and having a celebrity I think is cool think that I'm a loser is too devastating a possibility for me to bear.

So when Harry Styles came to New York, I was constantly on edge. I am normally not a person who experiences much FOMO, but with him even nominally "nearby" my levels were through the roof. Physical proximity lowered the otherwise insurmountable mountain of difference between us just enough to make me feel vaguely but defiantly optimistic that we could not only meet but get along. Sure, he was internationally famous, and a multimillionaire, and otherworldly handsome, and seven years my junior, among other complicating factors. But most of the time, he was all that plus an ocean (or more) away. When he came to New York, for five or ten days at a time, he was still all that, but we were in the same place. Geographically, there was at least a chance we could meet. In a city of 8.4 million people I became convinced I would run into him on the sidewalk with no one else around us.

Here's how it would happen: I'd turn the corner onto a quiet street around sunset, looking at my phone. I'd look up to make sure I wasn't about to run into anyone, and then I'd look back at my phone. But then, wait—I'd look up again. *Is that who I think . . .* way down at the other end of the street? No. I'd stop walking for a second, but only a second, because it would look weird if I froze for too long. We'd get close enough to each other to see each other and smile. He would see that I recognized him and would appreciate how chill I was being about it. "Excuse me," he'd say. "Which way is Allen Street?" Then there would be some stuff about directions, and this weird art thing he was trying to find because he had told a friend he'd go to it but really didn't want to go. I would say hey, that's not far from my favorite ice cream place. He would say ice cream sounds so much better than art right now. Then at some point after that he hugs me, and picks me up, and carries me over a threshold. I never worked out how we got to the ice cream place or where the threshold was or what was on the other side of it. That part didn't really matter. All I wanted was for him to hug me and then pick me up. I wanted to meet him so bad it made me nauseated.

Being at my desk at work during these visits was intolerable. Mackenzie and I would instant-message back and forth all day, sending links to pictures we'd found online of other, more blessed New Yorkers who'd run into Harry—*our* Harry—outside Veselka, or at the Met, or outside the Saint Laurent on Greene Street. Knowing he was that close, walking down streets I walked down all the time, while precious hours of possibility slipped away as I sat trapped at my desk, was torturous. At the beginning of every trip he made to New York, I felt so bright and full of hope, and by the end of every trip I was worn out, depressed, and deeply embarrassed. Mackenzie and I started saying we didn't want him to come to New York anymore, and we were only half-joking. It was simply too stressful.

But before we decided the best policy was to deliberately ignore Harry's presence in New York, we went to wait for him outside his hotel.

· · ·

In my defense, I'd had one prior experience that gave me reason to believe it could be that simple. Once, in the summer of 2006, my friends and I decided to go look for Lindsay Lohan in downtown Saint Paul, where she was on location for the film *A Prairie Home Companion*. Miracle of miracles, we actually *found* her, smoking a cigarette on the sidewalk outside her trailer—but that's a story for another time.

In Mackenzie's defense, let me make clear that this pursuit was largely my idea. Yes, she had a pretty good idea as to where Harry was staying—thanks to fan Twitter intel from previous visits, and a working knowledge on her part of the finer, chic-er New York City hotels—and yes, she could be talked into "dropping by" with me, but the responsibility for our loitering lies with me. I talked her into it. I said, "It's fine, we'll just stand there for two seconds. Just to see." She had some reservations about participating in what could fairly be called light stalking; I did not. It wasn't like I planned to try to get inside, or even talk to him. All I wanted was to stand on the sidewalk, twenty or thirty feet away from the hotel entrance, and see Harry either leave or return. Sure, in a dream world, maybe he'd wave. Blow a kiss. But I felt strongly that just seeing him would be enough. My One Direction fever would be broken, and I could return to a level of interest befitting an almost-thirty-year-old woman.

So Mackenzie and I left work around 6:00, walked out into a light rain, and headed south down Fifth Avenue. On the way there, under my umbrella, we worried aloud about the boys.

There was, by then, a vague sense that things might not continue on forever as they had. Most of the boys were staying at separate hotels when they toured, and video clips from their performances from the European leg showed them listless, distracted. Together we tried to prepare ourselves for the timeline ahead: the boys would record a fifth album, and then tour it, and then, probably, they'd be done. We thought this was more than reasonable. As adult fans we knew better than the teens who seemed to believe One Direction was incombustible and permanent. We'd seen the end of the Spice Girls and *NSYNC. We knew that nothing this beautiful and perfect could last.

But that night, that spring when Harry's hair was long but not yet too long, we were still hopeful. And when we rounded the corner onto West Third Street, and the Bowery Hotel came into view, my heart leapt into my throat.

The first thing I noticed was that we were not alone in our pursuit. This was not Minnesota. This was much bigger than Lindsay Lohan. Outside the entrance to the hotel there were four other clusters of girls that I could see, and we figured there were probably more around back. They huddled in smaller groups of two and three and four, some under umbrellas and some, more brave, sidled up alongside the building under the overhang. Two teenage girls were seated on a bench under a trellis, working on their laptops. *Oh my god*, I thought. *They are doing homework.*

As for Mackenzie and I, we stood as close as she was willing to go and as far away as I was willing to tolerate: about twenty yards. Without acknowledging what we were doing, we both pretended, on and off, to be looking up directions on our phones. I looked up now and again to watch hotel security watching the other girls, and each time a black car pulled up to the curb, I watched all ten or twelve of them freeze in place, their eyes glued to the back door. But it was never Harry who came out, and as soon as we accepted that, we resumed our collective charade. After fifteen minutes or so Mackenzie said we should go, but I negotiated her up to another fifteen. "Just think how we'll feel if we leave and find out he came out ten minutes later and hugged everybody," I said.

A few minutes later one of the clusters of girls abruptly walked around the corner to the side of the hotel. Then another group did.

"Something's happening," I said. Mackenzie and I stood there watching the other girls disappear, and then we panicked.

"What should we do?"

"I don't know."

"Should we follow them?"

"Where did they even go?"

"Maybe they know something we don't."

"Maybe he's coming out to say hi," said Mackenzie. I just about fainted.

"Oh my god, really?" I gasped. It was like I never heard the "maybe." *Harry Styles was coming out to say hi.* To us.

"Maybe," she repeated. "Like his manager could come out first and be like, you know, keep it cool, the ten of you can get a photo, but then you gotta go. I know it's definitely happened before."

I thought this made a lot of sense. Because we showed up and waited politely, we were going to be rewarded with meeting Harry Styles. As we rounded the corner my body started to shake. I imagined him coming out the side of the building, smiling at the line of girls waiting to see him. I imagined my turn and what I might say. I tried to plan a joke in advance, which is nearly impossible in the most optimal of circumstances. You can have it all mapped out, but rarely will the other person supply the setup your punch line requires, particularly when that person is a famous celebrity who doesn't know or care who you are. Still, I wanted to make an impact. I thought maybe I'd joke that we'd lined up not knowing what we were in line for. Something like, "Oh, we were just walking by and saw a line and thought maybe someone was giving away free food." I know that doesn't sound all that funny, but I was counting on my delivery to make it work.

Once we saw the other girls standing around what looked like a side entrance to the hotel, I lost whatever remaining shred of cool I had left. I texted Arianna to tell her I was about to meet Harry Styles, and she texted me back to say that if I met Harry Styles without her she would have to end our friendship. I was not insulted because I felt the same way. Maintaining a relationship under those conditions would be intolerable.

"When do you think he'll come out?" I asked Mackenzie. She shrugged. I was both impressed and annoyed by her blasé demeanor because I knew she was just as excited at the prospect of meeting Harry Styles as I was, if not more so. She was just better at not getting her hopes up. She refused to stand there staring at the door, so I stared at it for the both of us.

Ten or fifteen minutes passed and nothing happened. Then, one of the little groups of girls got up from their perch on a tree planter, wiped their hands across the backs of their jean shorts, and walked away. That they did so decisively gave me pause, but I comforted myself by telling myself that those four girls just made the biggest mistake of their lives.

Then another group left, too. All that remained were me, Mackenzie, and a group of teenagers waiting across the street.

"What should we do?" I asked.

"I dunno," said Mackenzie. "I'm not sure it's happening."

"I'm gonna ask those kids over there what's up," I said. Was I embarrassed by the prospect of approaching a group of teenagers, as a twenty-seven-year-old woman, to ask if they had any teenager-type intel into the whereabouts of my favorite boy-band member? Yes. So embarrassed. But I wasn't quite as embarrassed as I was desperate. If I was going to have spent an evening waiting for Harry Styles outside his hotel, then I wanted it to have been worth it. I crossed the street toward the girls, and Mackenzie followed reluctantly behind.

"Hi," I said. "Are you guys here because of Harry?" I whispered his name like it was a code word for drugs.

"Yeah," one of them said, and it was then that I saw she had braces.

"But we don't think he's here," said another. "At least, not anymore."

"Really??"

"Yeah," said Braces. "Someone who works at the hotel tweeted that he was here earlier so he had to move."

"Oh my god," I said. "That is so rude."

"I know."

I felt bad for Harry, but I felt even worse for me.

"Well, thanks for the tip," I said.

"No problem," said Braces.

"Can I ask how old you guys are?" I said.

"I'm sixteen," she said. "They're seventeen."

"Cool," I said. "I'm twenty-seven, and she's twenty-four." I half expected the girls to laugh at us, or throw up in shock, but they didn't. They got it. It was Harry Styles.

"I think we're gonna go try another hotel," said Braces, and I nodded solemnly, as if to say *good luck and godspeed*. There was a part of me that wanted to follow them, but there was a bigger part that knew it was time for me to concede. "Stopping by" a hotel that was "on the way home" from work in search of a young and famous celebrity was one thing, but following a group of teenagers to a second location was quite another. I texted Arianna to let her know we hadn't met Harry after all, and she texted back her condolences along with some barely camouflaged relief. I was not especially lucky after all. Perhaps you are allotted only a single planned and executed celebrity encounter in your lifetime, and I had wasted mine on Lindsay Lohan.

. . .

Less than a year after I loitered outside Harry Styles's hotel, One Direction began to fall apart. The news that Zayn had quit the band hit one morning when I was at work, and seconds after I saw the headline, a wailing chorus of "No!!" rang out through the office, and Mackenzie full-on ran from her desk to mine. Once there, she collapsed on the floor and pressed her hands over her face. We'd been preparing for this—Zayn had left the tour six days earlier for a "break," and before that had been skipping out on events and performances—but there is only so much you can do to get ready for something you don't really believe will happen. The longer I loved One Direction the more dreamy and rosy-eyed I'd become. First I loved them winkingly, and then sincerely, and then obsessively, and before I knew it their continued existence as an unbreakable unit was something I took for granted. I forgot to be cautious and cynical and instead gave myself over to hoping for the impossible. And in that way, loving One Direction made me a teenager again. The night Zayn left the band, I looked up "Goodbye Zayn"–type fan art on Tumblr. I found a drawing of Zayn hugging each of the other band members individually, their faces buried into his shoulder, their arms clasping his neck and back. Above them were written the words "I Love You So." I stared at this drawing and I sobbed my stupid teenage heart out.

My One Direction mania hit me hardest at a time when I was otherwise plagued by pessimism and gloom. It had been over a year and a half since I'd dated anyone, and it was only getting harder for me to remember how

I'd felt about those people before they hurt me and I decided I would hate them forever and never forgive them. My efforts (while admittedly modest) at "meeting someone new" hadn't gotten me anywhere, either. The last date I'd been on was with a guy I met on Tinder, and the main things we'd talked about were snuff films and his subway-tunnel-graffiti hobby. And this was the most appealing man I'd been able to find in months and months of swiping. I'd always known (or at least, been told) I was picky, but finding only a handful of men attractive seemed like something beyond just choosiness. But I didn't know what that something was. All I knew was that of the men available to me, there was almost no one I wanted, and with every person I swiped into the metaphorical trash can, it got harder and harder to believe I'd find one I did. The more time that went by, the more looking for love felt like a chore I hated, like dusting window blinds. I did it because I knew I was supposed to, and I knew I wanted its abstract outcome, but I wasn't having any fun.

Loving One Direction, though—that was fun. One Direction reminded me what it was like to like boys. Hand to heart, I swear I could get butterflies from looking at a GIF of Harry Styles's dimples. It was a sensation I seemed able to get only from media—a GIF, sure, or a movie, or a text or a Gchat from a guy I liked. But it had been years since I had felt that way about anyone in real life. Lately, when the opportunity for actual romance and actual sex presented itself, I found I no longer wanted it. For years I waited to kiss someone I actually truly liked, sure that then, finally, I'd feel the thing I was supposed to—the thing that was so conspicuously absent from

every drunken make-out I'd participated in throughout
college and the years afterward. But even when I finally
did kiss a man I really and truly liked, I felt almost nothing. All that was there was the feeling I get when I achieve
any task I set out to accomplish. That is to say, it definitely
felt as good as transferring a hundred dollars to my savings account, but not any better.

So maybe there really was something wrong with me.
And on the worst days, when I couldn't stop worrying it
was true, and my case was a hopeless one, and this was as
good as it was going to get, I listened to One Direction.
And, for a while, I forgot about men and thought instead
of the boys. The boys of 1D reminded me of the ones I
liked when I was in high school and college, but they were
even better, because of the grooming and the professional
stylists. Even better because they loved me as much as—
no, more than—I loved them. This was the message of
every last one of their songs. Through their sweepingly
romantic, comfortingly clichéd, and candy-sweet lyrics, I
was able to access my otherwise closed-off heart. I could
remember what it was like to ache for a boy I'd never met
and never would.

I have since learned that I am not the only gay girl to have
a massive crush on Harry Styles. In fact, I'd go so far as to
say that queer girls who are into Harry Styles is a definite
thing. The first clue came in the form of a recent email
from a thirty-year-old gay woman who met her girlfriend
through an informal but organized group of adult Harry
Styles fans. Prior to dating each other, neither woman had

dated women before, but both had loved Harry for a long time. I was intrigued. Not long ago I did an audit of my queer friends at work and realized that at least three or four were or are obsessed with Harry, too. So were several of the queer women online whom I've made friends with based on shared queerness and interest in Harry Styles. (One of them, Fran, has the same sad and Zayn-less One Direction calendar as me, and we both post pictures of it on the first of each month.) Ruby Tandoh, the out cookbook author and former *Great British Bake Off* contestant, is a professed fangirl. Jane Lynch has even talked about her crush on Harry, and she is both gay and fifty-seven years old. It doesn't matter. Harry is perfect. He is for everyone.

I guess what I'm trying to say is that I think Harry Styles has the power to make women realize they're queer, but that sounds bad. That sounds like the premise of a rom-com formed by cutting and pasting together scraps from the screenplays for *Gigli* and *Good Luck Chuck*. I do not mean Harry Styles is a turn-off so strong that the mere sight of him could turn a straight woman gay; rather, I mean that his own boyish, beautiful androgyny has served as a linchpin for many young (and even youngish) women who grew up liking boys but find themselves unable to muster the same adoration for most men. We see Harry, with his long, curly hair, flowy silk shirts, his tight, women's Paige-brand jeans, his stacked-heel boots, and we think: *I want that.* We want him and his clothes. We want to hold him and we want to be him.

Harry Styles was one of my last and biggest stumbling blocks when it came to figuring out my sexuality. I

thought, *How can I like girls if I like Harry Styles this much?*
How could someone with as many photos of Harry Styles
saved to her iPhone's camera roll as I had not want to end up
with, barring the very small likelihood of Harry himself, at
least a man? I could so vividly imagine being held by him,
squeezed by him, picked up and carried over that threshold. Sure, I kind of blanked on what should happen after
that. But that was only because I didn't have enough experience.

When I came out to Chiara, I told her that I still
didn't know what exactly I was. I said I was actively talking to girls on dating apps, but that I was confused because I still loved Harry Styles more than anyone. This
conversation happened on Gchat, where Chiara had the
annoying (but endearing) habit of typing only a word or
two before hitting Enter, such that each sentence is split
into several lines. She wrote:

I mean
Harry Styles
kind of
. . .
looks like
. . . a lesbian.

I laughed. She was not wrong. And I hope I'm not
mistaken, but I have this feeling that if Harry Styles was
to read this book (just let me have this dream) and he saw
what Chiara and I had said about him here, he would be
flattered. Why shouldn't he be? Lesbians are hot. So is
Harry Styles.

. . .

I saw One Direction for the second and final time in August 2015, in New Jersey, as part of their On the Road Again tour. So much had changed between the first One Direction concert I went to and this one. The second time around, we had this foreboding sense (though not yet confirmed) that this could very well be the last time we ever saw the band perform. A little over a month earlier, I'd come out to my friends. And, just a week after that, I had met Lydia. On the day after our first date, at some point in a daylong texting marathon, she texted me a GIF of Harry Styles. I flipped. I asked her if she knew what she was doing by sending me that GIF—I didn't think I'd gushed about 1D on our date, but consuming two gin-and-tonics without dinner made me less than positive. She texted back that no, I hadn't told her how much I loved Harry or One Direction. She'd used the GIF because everyone at home used to call her Styles because they had the same exact haircut and looked alike. She told me her mom sometimes texted her paparazzi photos of Harry from *Us Weekly* and captioned them "I thought this was you." Then she sent me a picture of herself in college to prove it, and my mouth fell open. I heard the "Hallelujah Chorus" in my head. I had found the lesbian Holy Grail I hadn't even known I was searching for: a girl who looks like Harry Styles. Three weeks later—not because of this similarity, but not in spite of it, either—we were girlfriends.

To what I assume was the last One Direction concert of my life, I wore a T-shirt (again made by Matt) that, at my request, said: "947 Times Harry Styles and Katie Heaney Defined Relationship Goals," with "BuzzFeed" printed underneath in red. Lydia was a pretty good sport about it. She did not *love* how much I loved Harry Styles, but if I was going to harbor an infatuation with a male celebrity, better that it be for one who looked like her.

If I arrived at the first concert a lukewarm, half-ironic fan, I arrived at this one a full-on 1D maniac. This time, we had much, much better seats. We were the oldest people in our section by at least eight years, but I didn't care. I felt grateful for my age and the extra height it provided me. While we waited for the show to start, we watched roadies walk to the end of the catwalk to set things up and squealed, "*Ohmygod,* Harry's going to be that close."

When the boys finally came onstage, I cried. There was this overwhelming sense of survival in their being here, despite a hard year, despite losing someone we had loved. The crowd was not just overjoyed but grateful. It felt like we knew the end was near, but that was probably me projecting. Because I was older than almost everybody there who wasn't some preteen's dad, I was therefore slightly more aware of mortality. The girls were still hoping for their miracle to last forever. When the band played "18," one of my very favorite songs, they all held up signs, echoing the lyrics, that said, "I Have Loved You Since I Was ____." Most of them said 11, 13, 14, 16. Had I gotten the memo, and I wished I had, mine would have said, I have loved you since I was twenty-six. It is never too late.

10

WHAT NOT TO WEAR

Two hours after I came out to my mom over the phone, she called me back with a follow-up question: "Are you still going to wear dresses?"

I thought this was funny, and sweet. It was funny because it was so Mom, but even more so because I loved dresses. I laughed. "Yes!!" I assured her. Of course I would still wear them. I was exactly the same person as before. Right?

About a month later I flew back home to Minnesota for my ten-year high school reunion, and my mom and I went shopping. I bought a sundress that was emerald-green—my favorite color. It was a little too daytime-beachside-barbecue for my reunion, but I texted a picture of me wearing it to Lydia, and she texted back a series of heart-eyes emojis, so I decided to buy it anyway. I packed it into my suitcase, flew back to Brooklyn, and hung it up in my closet, where it remained, untouched, for more than a year.

I've worn a dress a few times since then—to a fundraiser cocktail party in muggy early September, on some other ordinary day too hot to consider allowing fabric to touch my inner thighs—but somehow, at some point, without realizing that a shift was taking place until it was complete, something horrible happened: I proved my mother right. I stopped wanting to wear dresses. I was not exactly the same person as before.

I didn't really notice anything was up until fall came, and suddenly one of my favorite easy workday looks—a sweater over a skirt with tights and boots—no longer appealed to me. Something just looked . . . off. All my skirts were too poufy, and the dresses hung lifelessly off my body. I looked too girly. As someone who, at least until then, liked to look somewhat girly, at least some of the time—someone who regularly browsed Anthropologie's sale section, who'd pictured Kevin Costner's wife's giant, billowing wedding dress as the platonic ideal of wedding dresses since 2004—this was disorienting to me. I chalked it up to the normal ups and downs of dressing oneself, vowing to try the offending outfit again a few days later. But then that day would come, and it still didn't look, or feel, right.

It was a strange feeling to miss my dresses as they hung, unharmed and available, in my closet. The only thing stopping me from wearing them was me. I wished I still wanted to wear them, but I didn't. I didn't want new ones for a long time, either, and because of that, an entire window of shopping possibility was closed on me.

It wasn't just dresses and skirts, either; I lost entire stores. My Internet browser's search bar still auto-filled the names of former favorites—Madewell, H&M, J.Crew, LOFT, all the places I'd almost always been able to find something I wanted. But after I stopped looking at their dresses, I noticed myself losing interest in their other clothes, too. Suddenly it all looked so . . . heterosexual.

Maybe it's silly to grieve my lost appreciation for mass-market retailers, but not knowing where to shop made me sad, because I love to shop. I was not looking to adopt some sort of Marie Kondo–esque Zen state in which I accepted simplicity and minimalism into my life. I would have preferred to have a shit ton of clothes I loved. I would have preferred to be so overwhelmed by choice that I had to plan my outfits in advance. In my senior year of high school, my best friend and I had a competition to see who could go the longest into the year without repeating an outfit. She won, but I made it into early November.

After I came out, my clothing overwhelmed me, for sure, but not because there was too much of it to choose from. I felt overwhelmed by opening my closet and seeing clothes I couldn't even remember wanting. I felt overwhelmed when I ran my hand over the soft silk of my dresses and wondered whether I should donate them, or keep them, just in case I changed again. I was overwhelmed by the pervasive sense of in-betweenness I felt—not yet ready to let go, unsure how to move forward.

· · ·

After a lifetime of feeling left out of my friends' dating conversations by my perpetual singleness, I'd looked forward to getting all caught up and included once I got into a relationship of my own. Then I realized: I'll never be caught up. I'll never have experienced teenage love, and I'll never have had the kind of sexy early-twenties hijinks so many of my friends had. I entered my first relationship at twenty-eight, and it was with a woman, and almost all my friends are straight, and it's not completely different, but it's different enough. I've talked about guys with my friends all my life, but in coming out I felt I'd waived the extremely small amount of street cred I had. And most of the queer friends I'd made had all been out much longer than I had, and around them, I didn't feel gay enough. I was suddenly underqualified for everything.

So I felt adrift. Like everybody else, I was convinced I was singularly, hopelessly, particularly alone in my circumstances. There wasn't a lot to do about it apart from continuing to allow time to pass. I hoped I'd eventually lose interest in my own queerness in favor of something else, like, I don't know, artisanal bread baking. But for most of that entire first year, being gay was the most important thing about me, to me, and I was frustrated by my inability to telegraph this change through my clothing.

As my identity shifted, so, too, did the audience I had in mind when I got dressed. While I still wanted my straight friends to think I looked great, I really, really wanted my queer friends to think I looked great. I also just wanted to look queer. At least more so. At least enough so that when I saw a pair of lesbians on the street in Brooklyn, it was possible they would look at me and recognize me as a card-carrying member of the club.

While I knew that queer women can wear any style they want and be no more or less queer because of it, I also knew there were some signifiers. But my tattoos were minimal, and my face unpierced; I was pretty sure I lacked the edge to pull off daytime sweatpants, and most hats just look stupid on me. If I wanted to look a little gayer at a formal event, I could wear a suit instead of a dress. But on ordinary days (which was most of them), I couldn't figure out how to look both a little gayer and like myself.

When I started dating Lydia, I used to watch over her shoulder while she browsed her favorite online store on her phone. (So soothing, like watching someone else play a video game you've never played and never will.) First I noticed the prices: they were suspiciously low.

"Is that in American dollars?!" I yelled.

"Yup," she said. "Men's clothing. It's ridiculous."

I watched for another couple of minutes in silence. Then:

"Wait! I like that shirt!!"

So, because it was only eight dollars, my girlfriend bought it for me. It was a black short-sleeved T-shirt, but the crew neck was high, and the sleeves long enough to roll up, the way I liked. I downloaded the store's app to my own phone, and began cautiously injecting a bit of menswear into my closet. It wasn't easy. For one thing, most men's clothing is boring. You just don't see a male equivalent of, like, peplum. There was a way to look cool

in simple combinations of pants and T-shirts and jackets—
I'd seen it done again and again on the various tomboy
fashion Instagrams I followed—but I could never figure it
out for myself.

While it was confusing to grow disconnected from so
much of the clothing I once loved, it was also exciting to
imagine what might take its place. It was a slow process
(which was good for my bank account, at least), and often
a frustrating one. Sometimes, rudely, the things that
looked cool on hot Instagram models did not look all that
cool on me. Many of the things I ordered online, warily
and hopefully, I returned. Successes were few, but invigorating: a hooded black spring jacket, men's and therefore
maybe the first jacket I've owned with sleeves long enough
for my arms; a pair of black sneakers that went on my feet
like glass slippers. (If there's one thing that remained con-
stant, it was a heavy preference for black.)

In the early spring after I started dating Lydia, I at-
tempted to clean out my closet. This was something I
should have done months earlier, regardless of seasonal
appropriateness—it was messy, full of things I hadn't
worn in ages. Getting rid of things is hard for me. When
I went off to college, I nearly cried throwing out my JV
tennis T-shirts, and they were sweat-stained and hideous.
But you have to let go of former selves to make space for
new ones.

Though I was able to clean out and donate a few large
garbage bags' worth of clothing, I held on to the green
dress through the summer, just in case. But I didn't wear
it once. I didn't even think about wearing it. In the fall,
when my roommate Rachel organized a clothing swap, I

put my green dress up for the taking. Nobody took it. The rejection of one's clothing is always humiliating (see: every consignment experience I've ever had), but this felt almost taunting. It wasn't until December that I finally got rid of it. A co-worker of mine offered to gather up Christmas clothing donations at our office, so I brought it to work and left it neatly folded in the big cardboard donation box beside her desk.

But by then something strange was happening—I was starting to like some of the old standbys again. My eyes no longer glazed over when I went to browse Madewell or H&M online. The things I liked were maybe not exactly the things I liked before, but these shifts in taste have always happened to me periodically, gay or not. I still do not feel particularly inclined toward dresses or skirts, but I no longer feel like that is due to anything more than a passing trend or whim. Not long after my men's short-sleeved button-up phase, I got really into blazers and silk blouses and skinny trousers—a look I more or less stole from *How I Met Your Mother*'s Robin Scherbatsky, and thus named "the off-duty newscaster." It was structured but femme, the kind of outfit a women's magazine would call "borrowed from the boys." It was not particularly fashion-forward, or interesting, but I have lately come to accept that my style may never be particularly fashion-forward or interesting.

Recently I told Lydia that I was kind of over my boy-clothes phase, and she smiled knowingly, which of course annoyed me. I knew what she'd say—that I'd gone through the same thing so many queer women go through when they first come out. I'd done the stereo-typical Baby Dyke thing of buying a bunch of men's shirts and snapback hats and whatever else I saw all the Instagram lesbians wearing, and had tried in earnest to make them fit me. And then, slowly but surely, I turned back into myself: a not-all-that-stylish copycat who vac-illates between tomboy and femme, depending on the day. I dyed my hair back to something like my natural medium brown from its former bleached blond. I bought some silk shirts and a chicly shapeless dress. I got this unexpected urge to wear heels—just once, and I was all set again for the next year.

I would have loved to come out and feel at once fully formed, somehow done as a person. For a while I felt a real comfort in knowing that my clothing said some-thing about the person I'd so recently become. But after a while being capital-g Gay lost some of its novelty, and became instead just one of the many things that make me who I am. The clothing I'd acquired in an attempt to fit a self-imposed mold—clothing I really did want, the kind of clothing I still admire on other people—started feeling as weird on my body as the green dress before it. I have given most of my wannabe tomboy costumes to Lydia, who conveniently wears the same size shirts that I do.

I am trying to accept a winnowed wardrobe made up mostly of basics. After all, there has really been only one outfit that has remained equally comfortable throughout this whole process, and that is a black sweatshirt with black jeans. In this outfit I feel as at peace as I did as a third grader in Catholic school, wearing my uniform, a navy sweatshirt over navy leggings. But even I get bored of being boring sometimes, and that is when I am most prone to pursuing a new look. Perhaps one day I will really nail it, and become known for my trademark hairstyle, or glasses, or high-top tennis shoes. Until then, I will probably continue taking cues from Kristen Stewart.

Girl #4

Shakira, eighth grade—?? I learned of Shakira in my eighth grade Spanish 1 class, which was my favorite class that year. Before class began, my teacher played Spanish-language pop, and I always got there early to hear it. After hearing songs from *Pies Descalzos* so many times, I asked my teacher who sang it, and she handed me Shakira's CD to take home over the weekend so I could burn myself a copy. For the rest of middle school it was all I listened to. With allowance money I bought Shakira's *MTV Unplugged* DVD and watched her belly dance in leather pants in my family's living room, feeling vaguely embarrassed whenever my mom or dad walked through the room. For my birthday I asked for a two-by-three-foot poster of her, and when it arrived I hung it on the wall above my dresser, where it stayed until I went off to college.

11

I.O.U.

The first time I posted a picture of Lydia and me on Instagram, I instantly wondered if the strangers who followed me because of my first book would be able to tell she and I were dating. It was a selfie taken from above, the two of us lying next to each other on the floor of the American Museum of Natural History below the fiberglass giant blue whale suspended above. We are not kissing, or even touching, but neither is the photo overtly platonic. So, of course they could tell. I know now that it's always obvious. But at the time, it seemed too sharp a turn for anyone to follow. Throughout the first few months of my relationship with Lydia, my dual existence as the private, present me versus the previous self I'd made public was rarely far from my mind.

I knew my sexuality was something I'd have to write about, and would want to write about, eventually, but I was also superstitious, and worried that making some huge announcement might somehow cause my relationship to fall apart. I worried about claiming a label only to end up shedding it months or years later. I worried I'd lost credibility as an authority on myself. I knew I had to say something, but I didn't want to say anything, for fear of making myself inaccurate.

This sense of confessional responsibility is one of the strangest things about being a semi–public figure, and I've experienced it only on a very small scale. Before I wrote my first book, nobody who didn't know me personally cared about me—as it should be. And judging by the ratio of people who contacted me about my book to people who read it, most of the latter felt it contained as much information about me as they could possibly need. If not more. But there was a subset of people who had a follow-up question for every confession I shared. Most were kind and simply curious—the emails that asked if I had found a boyfriend since writing, and if not, how I was doing. But occasionally they went deeper. Once, a young woman messaged me on Facebook to ask if I could send her pictures of everyone I described in the book. I was shocked and offended by her nerve.

The thing is, I'm a hypocrite. I found this girl's message creepy, but I once tracked down the LinkedIn page of a woman who was dating a semi-famous lesbian YouTuber so I could learn her age. I didn't know either of these people. I will probably never meet them. I don't particularly *want* to meet them. Their lives are not especially interesting, aside from the fact that they seem to have a lot of money. The YouTube model of fame makes me feel elderly and alien, and yet—I get sucked in. I refer to them by first name. I gossip about their relationships as if I know them. So help me god, I "ship." I do not think of these people as entirely *real*. They exist only as I know them, in snippets, through the beautifully filtered lens of Instagram.

If there is a line between curious fan behavior and creepy fan behavior, it is hazy, and suited to my own needs. I would never email a stranger to ask her about her divorce, but I will try to put together a timeline of her relationship's demise using her social media platforms. I arrive at the end of these information-gathering sessions bewildered and embarrassed. I do not know why I care. I only know that my desire to pry is bottomless. I want to collect every sordid detail of every life that I possibly can. It is as if I think knowing more about other people's lives will preserve my own.

Still, I have never wanted answers about a stranger's life so badly that I have asked the source herself. I'm too self-conscious, and too proud; I couldn't bear to have anyone famous or even sort of famous think I care that much about them. Obviously, though, I do.

What does any of us owe anyone else? I want to say: nothing, not one thing to anyone. But that would be me pretending to be much more of an individualist than I really am. Like most Catholics, former or present, I envy all hedonists. Every single one of my days is engineered toward the completion of a lifelong checklist. A lot of the time I can't tell if I'm doing something because I think I should or because I really want to. It is depressing to think that for me, maybe, those two must always overlap. The worst part is that I'm not even religious, and so, presumably, there is no heaven waiting as a reward for all this good behavior.

The fact is that I *do* feel as though I owe something to anyone who cares enough about me to read my books or follow me online. I wouldn't necessarily say the same must be true for other writers or artists, but if you put work into the world hoping for an audience, I think it's unreasonable to expect that relationship to remain entirely one-sided. If I didn't want to know what anyone thought of my work, I wouldn't publish it. If I didn't want people to know personal details about my life, this would be a pretty funny way of showing it. I may not have known what exactly I was in for when I published my first book, but it is only because people responded to it the way they did that I am here now. There is responsibility there, even if there are days I don't want it.

So when I'd been dating Lydia for a little over three months, and that didn't seem likely to change anytime soon, I came out to the Internet. I wrote:

> I have a girlfriend now; there's no reason to bury the lede, especially when it's maybe not even as much of a lede as I think it is. That, really, has been the main reason for my reticence. Part of me is like "Shut upppp, who CARES" and part of me is like "well, what if everybody does?????"
>
> I wrote a decently popular book about wanting (and failing) to date boys, and now I am dating a girl, and will maybe only ever date girls. Singular or plu-

ral, who knows. If I have learned anything from the various epiphanies that have occurred to me in the nearly two years since my book came out—my book, in which I claim to know myself very well—it is that I am able to be certain of much less than I thought when I was a little younger than I am now.

Maybe this isn't a huge contradiction like I sometimes fear. Reactions to my news have been almost disappointingly nonchalant. I kept telling my therapist, "I feel like there should have been more crying." An interrogation, at least! Instead, most everyone I've told was like "Huh!" and then they were like ". . . Huh."

Telling strangers is different, though—both easier and more overwhelming. Easier because I do not necessarily care what any one of them thinks, but more overwhelming in that, together, they are a much larger group than people who know me personally. If one girl who read my book and felt we were the same—even though that was never all the way true, because no two people are—was to now feel disappointed to find out we are not, I would perhaps feel a tiny loss, but I would be fine. If many of them were to feel that way, I would feel that I had let a group of people I care about down. I wanted to be a role model, sort of, and then I think I was, and it has been both gratifying and strange. Now I just want to be myself again. I told my therapist I wanted there to be two me's: one for myself, who can keep everything in some protected, real-life bubble, and another for strangers, to carry on as the Katie they believe they

know. (This is all obviously narcissistic. Two of me!
I'm practically making myself throw up.)

Or, I guess what I want is for there to still be
someone like the me I presented in that book—
unlucky in (hetero) love, but plucky and resilient and
optimistic about what her future looks like—so that
the girls who needed her still have her. Because I get
that; I wanted that. I always wanted to see some version of me who was living my life (the outline of it, at
least) but three or four years ahead, so I could know
that I was normal, and okay, and that I'd be happy.
When I was younger I looked for a straight girl still
single (but happy!) at twenty or twenty-five or thirty,
and later I looked for a queer girl who didn't "know"
until late, in all the same ways I didn't and then did,
and I never found either one. Now I know that's because neither of them is really there. I'm not exactly
that girl for anyone else, either, and I'm sorry—not
because I want to be any different but because I know
what it's like to feel alone.

Probably my biggest fear is that girls who felt less
alone because of my book will now feel it seeping
back, even though that was never really in my power
to prevent. My second biggest fear is that people will
look from my book to me now and back again and
go, *Oh, well that's why.* I don't think it's that simple.
I told the truth as best I could and now the truth is
a little bigger.

I've been going back and forth for a while on
whether I should "say something" about this, in a
more public sense, because I am pretty much con-

stantly torn between wanting to never write about my personal life ever again and wanting to do only that, and I expect this push and pull to continue for basically the rest of my annoying life. But as much as I'm nagged by these fears about vague, hypothetical complications resulting from my book and my online persona and the ways I have changed and will continue to change, I'm much more bothered by the idea of not saying something online simply because I am afraid. It is very likely that there is a more thoughtful way to say most of this, but I am beginning to think that thoughtfulness can be overdone, and that after a certain amount of time spent thinking and thinking and thinking things over it might be better to just finally say the thing you've been wondering if you should say, and see what happens next.

I didn't know exactly what to expect when I came out online. I tried to publish that post before I could think about it too much. I was afraid that people would think I was a hypocrite, or a liar, or an idiot. I didn't want the many kind people who'd read my first book and told me I mattered to them to now decide that I didn't. I didn't want people telling me I should have known sooner. I hate uncertainty, and I really hate being late, and here I was, guilty of both. But as is usually the case, I shouldn't have spent so much time worrying. The responses were so overwhelmingly supportive that even now, more than two years later, I find it hard to articulate how much they mean to me. I'd struggled to explain how I'd changed so much in such a short time, and women I didn't even know were there to tell me there was no explanation necessary. They told me it made sense. That *I* made sense. My story didn't have to fit inside anyone's expectations, because it wasn't, first and foremost, a story. It was my life.

My first book was true. So is this one.

People want a clear narrative arc. Especially me. We want gay adults to have gay childhoods—the elementary school crushes, the closeted adolescence, the gradual coming to terms. We want a line, no breaks, no swerving, from point A to point B. But I broke and I swerved plenty. I feel behind, but I truly didn't know how to get here any quicker. I didn't even know where I was trying to go. In every moment leading up to this one, at ages nine and fourteen and nineteen and twenty-six, I have been as close to myself as I knew how to be. I may know myself better now than I ever have before, but ask me again in a year or two.

12

INTROVERT PROBLEMS

The first time I was prescribed an anti-anxiety medication, I was at the tail end of a three-week frantic hypochondria episode during which I convinced myself I had both a heart condition and elephantiasis of the foot. The foot thing is a long story, or at least it seemed grounded in a long and plausible medical history to me at the time. I'd had some problems with it in college, some off-and-on pain and swelling, which I chalked up to my illustrious career as a Division III tennis team bench-warmer. It went away, but then, a few years later, bored at the office where I was working as a summer policy intern, I looked at my feet beneath my desk and noticed one of them was . . . fat. I spun out very quickly from there—within hours I was on Web forums and self-diagnosing.

Within days I was ordering obscure supplements meant to relieve inflammation off the Internet. I took my own pulse twenty times a day, convinced my heart was about to beat out of my chest. I was pretty sure my foot would need to be amputated.

I knew I was experiencing anxiety, but I also believed I was gravely ill, because there was no way anxiety alone could make me feel this bad. I told my supervisor I needed to finish my internship from home. I kept developing new symptoms. My entire left side started to tingle: on top of everything else, I was having a multiday stroke. One night, around 4:00 A.M., I called the nurse helpline on the back of my insurance card to ask if she thought I should go to the E.R. Among other diagnostics, she told me to pick up a cup with my left hand. If it didn't fall to the floor, she said, I probably wasn't having a stroke. I walked into my bathroom and picked up my blue ceramic toothbrush holder and held on for dear life. But even when it didn't fall, I didn't really believe I was okay.

I went to urgent care the next morning and told a doctor about my many worrying symptoms. She took my vitals and poked my swollen foot and looked deep into my pupils, but not until I admitted to my anxiety did she have any answers. As soon as I did, it was like I'd said the magic word. She wrote me a prescription for twenty milligrams of Celexa, which I traded for Lexapro two weeks later after I didn't feel any better. On Lexapro I experienced little to no side effects apart from a vague sense that I felt a bit too even-keeled. Nothing much bothered me, which . . . bothered me. I missed my sometimes-frantic energy, and I began to forget what it had felt like to be in one's dominating trait, which is confusing for me. I always wanted to be more outgoing, more commanding a presence, louder, more socially skilled. The life of the party. Nobody has ever described me as the life of the party. I am lucky if I get "I'm pretty sure she was there." I arrive early and leave early. I don't drink very much. I have lost my tolerance for existing with a hangover, and I feel like I had more than enough alcohol in college to last a lifetime. During those years I had a few shining moments in which I was, if not the most popular person at the party, the loudest. After a number of tequila shots that would probably kill me today, I would make myself known—running home from the bar, screaming my way through a frat house, starting a dance floor in an inopportune location.

Today, somehow, the cool thing (I'm basing this on the Internet) is to be hot and sad and alone. I would say I grew up at the wrong time, but I was not a hot and sad teenager, either. (Alone, sure.) I've never had the kind of lips one needs to make one's forlorn Instagram selfies pop. There is nothing mysterious or sexy or troubled about my wish to stay home alone. I'm just kind of boring. I love going to bed by 10:00 with my makeup washed off and my teeth brushed and flossed. I think a lot of people thrive off the unpredictability of going to one party and then another, but I hate it. Every time I'm about to go out and talk to people, I act like I've never talked to anyone before in my life. Seeing people I know well enough to greet but not well enough to maintain a reserve of conversation topics with stresses me out. I would rather stay home than have to think up a normal question I can ask someone after "how are you" and "how's work" and "do you know where the bathroom is." I treat every social gathering like a bomb I can only defuse by rigorous anticipatory worrying. I don't think any of these introverted tendencies are particularly great qualities to have, so I'm not sure why anyone brags about them. If a genie were to grant me three wishes, I would wish for world peace, universal student-loan debt forgiveness, and some sort of pendant or ring that would make me into a social butterfly whenever I wore it.

If there is one exception to my general distaste for big social gatherings, it is the formal dance. As a senior in high school I brought a picture of *The O.C.*'s Summer Roberts to my hairstylist and asked her to make my prom hair look like that, and little has changed since. I look forward to these rare and glamorous occasions like a lesser Austen sister looks forward to a ball. Thus, a few years ago, the night before my then-employer's holiday party—which I couldn't help but refer to as "the dance"—I found myself again at the hairstylist with a picture in my hand: "It's My Life"–era Gwen Stefani. My hair was bleached platinum blond then, too, and I was wearing a tuxedo jumpsuit, and I thought finger waves and red lipstick would pull the whole thing together perfectly. And it had to be perfect because, for the first time ever, I had an actual, romantic date to a formal event: Lydia and I had started dating a few months earlier.

When I woke up the next morning, and took out the dozens of pins my hairstylist had set my hair in, my hair did not look like Gwen Stefani's hair. If anything, it looked more like Bon Jovi's "It's My Life"–era hair. And from there it was all downhill—not because anything went that badly, but because already, as soon as I woke up, my mile-high expectations had failed me. My jumpsuit didn't fit like I wanted it to. I had a headache. My three-inch heels already hurt. By the time I met Lydia at the venue I was irretrievably crabby, which made her crabby with me in return, which made me even crabbier. I gulped down two gin-and-tonics, which for me, in those days, was enough to cause a scene. Lydia tried to make me dance and I refused. Apparently, once it became clear the night was not going to be the most magical night of my life, I decided instead to behave like a drunken Real Housewife at a fundraiser for underprivileged ponies. I pulled my friend Arianna away from her boyfriend to vent incoherently about nothing. I stomped my way over to the treat table, where I huffily assembled a plate of red and green Rice Krispies Treats and ate them one after another. Later that night, Lydia and I took a row of very cute photo-booth pictures in which you cannot tell I am still seething, which is a miracle.

The longer Lydia and I have been together, the easier it has gotten for me to let her talk me through one of my tailspins. Usually, she sees them coming on before I do. She likes to lift my arms above my head as I breathe in, and lower them as I breathe out. I always feel stupid. It always helps.

But I am stubborn, so it has taken me ages. I still don't

particularly like having my anxiety pointed out to me—
it's only okay when I say it. Coming from anyone else, I
tend to interpret "anxious" as invalidating, as an insult. If
Lydia suggested I take half a Xanax in the midst of a panic
attack, what I heard was: I can't handle you, and clearly
you can't handle yourself. I did not see anxiety or depres-
sion as a sign of weakness in other people, but I used to see
them that way in myself. I wasn't supposed to need anyone or anything. *I didn't have this problem when I was
single,* I thought. When I later said the same thing to my
therapist, she pointed out that I was plenty anxious when
I was single, too. The only difference was that then there
was nobody around to notice.

Some months after the holiday party, after a number
of needless, inexplicable pre-party arguments with Lydia,
and much internal debate, I asked my therapist if she
thought it might be time for me to try a new medication.
Broaching the subject was like pulling my own teeth.
Being independent all those years had made me self-
assured to the point that, for a long time, I insisted upon
my anxiety and my social skittishness as integral parts of
my personality. To seek medical intervention for them
was to admit I was faulty, which to me felt like the kind
of concession advice columnists are always telling you not
to make. I had always relied very heavily on the mantra
"Be yourself." Now I wonder: How many of us are so great
that being exactly ourselves is the best we can possibly be?

My therapist prescribed me twenty milligrams of Pro-
zac, to be taken once a day. I have taken it faithfully for
nearly two years and I don't intend to stop taking it anytime soon, if ever. I feel so much better that I hate to think

Girl #5

· ·

Andrea Carson from the Disney Channel original movie *Motocrossed*, age fifteen. A (very) loose adaptation of Shakespeare's *Twelfth Night*, *Motocrossed* is the story of a girl named Andrea who just wants to ride bikes, but because her dad thinks motocross isn't for girls, she must do so in secret. But then, her brother gets injured before a big race, so Andrea, unbeknownst to her family, cuts her hair short like a boy's and enters the race in her brother's place. There are a few scenes in which other girls, believing "Andi" to be a boy, are shown flirting with her, and it wasn't hard to see why. Even for a Disney Channel original movie, it was intensely homoerotic.

13

PRIDE

Not long after Lydia and I started dating, I went home with her to San Diego for a Thanksgiving vacation. She gave me a tour of the neighborhood where she grew up—the middle school and high school, the soccer field where she'd been the star player, the hill she Rollerbladed down so fast she had to dive into a bush to stop herself. The older she got, the further all her personal historic landmarks took us from her mother's house. Once we got into her early twenties, we drove into Hillcrest, the city's gay neighborhood, and there she took me to a lesbian bar called Gossip Grill.

"Gossip Girl?" I said.

"Gossip Grill."

I'd been in gay bars several times before—with a

friend of mine, in college, as an ostensibly straight woman who just wanted to dance—but never to a specifically lesbian one. I was nervous. For one thing, Lydia had told me this was where she used to hang out with her ex and their friends. They had, in fact, had the first of their two breakups on the bar's dance floor on Saint Patrick's Day. (Ah, to be young!) Though it was a Tuesday night, we were both steeling ourselves for the possibility of a run-in. Walking up to the bar in the dark, I felt like I was approaching a haunted house.

But it wasn't just the spectral ex that I was afraid of. I was also afraid that the lesbians in the lesbian bar would see me and realize that I did not belong there. Never mind that I was wearing, on purpose, the gayest outfit I owned (a tropical-print short-sleeved shirt buttoned all the way up, black skinny jeans, high-top tennis shoes), or that I was there with the woman I was sleeping with. I still felt like a fake. I was freshly twenty-nine, and I'd been gay for a grand total of five months. My heart beat fast in my chest as I handed the female bouncers my ID, and I worried, as I have worried every time I've entered a bar since I turned twenty-one, that I would be refused entry. Only this time, I wasn't worried it would be because my hair was a different color from the photo or because, unbeknownst to me, I was actually underage and not almost thirty. Instead, I imagined the woman who grabbed my ID taking a brief look at it, and another at my face, and saying, "Sorry. Not gay enough."

Obviously, this did not happen. The bouncers did not care any more about me than they did anyone else they let in. While Lydia got us each a drink, I scanned the room, bar that used to be her lesbian bar, I wondered how I measured up to the girl who used to sit in my place. Lydia's friends were very nice to me. Some more than others, maybe, but no one was rude, and no one ignored me. Everyone asked me what I did for work and where I was from, and as usual I was so focused on trying to make myself seem friendly that I forgot to ask enough questions in return. I was trying too hard to hear everything that everyone around me was saying to focus on any one of them. One of the girls there had apparently broken up with a long-term girlfriend only a few months earlier and, according to the others, was now hooking up with every twenty-two-year-old girl she could find. Another of them, the one I knew to be the ex's best friend, talked about her long-distance relationship with a woman who lived in Australia, and another, who was evidently in love with that best friend, complained about a girl who'd recently stopped texting her. I felt like a freak then, and I feel like one now, retelling it, because I was a little too rapt, and too wide-eyed, and I worried I was staring. Even after I'd come out, I was fascinated by lesbians being lesbians and talking about lesbians, to a degree that didn't seem fitting for someone who now identified as one herself. *Everyone around me is a woman talking about sleeping with women!!!* I wanted to yell. *Is everyone hearing this???* I still couldn't quite believe a place full of people like these ones existed, and I still couldn't quite believe I was one of them.

When we left the bar a little over an hour later, I wanted to know everything about everyone we'd met and their relationships past and present. In bed that night I looked most of them up on Instagram because I wanted to see what everyone they'd talked about looked like, because I was then—and am still—getting used to the idea that there isn't any one particular way that queer women look. Lydia did her best to humor me and answer my many detailed questions, but for her, this wasn't some fascinating new world she'd only just entered. She'd been there for almost fifteen years. To her, this was normal. I asked her if she missed her hometown queer scene, and she said yes, sometimes. Not so much that bar in particular (though that, too), and not all the individual people she left behind, but the sense of community she felt when she was there with them. It's a belongingness I haven't really gotten to experience, the kind I've been searching for ever since.

A few weeks before I met Lydia, the company where I worked had a big party for Pride Week. Although I'd only really come out to two friends from work (and even then not as gay or bisexual, but as someone who was thinking about it and would get back to you in 7–365 business days), when I walked into that party I was surprised to find I felt like I truly belonged there. Even if nobody else there knew it, I did. My friends and I got drinks at the bar, then gathered around a jar full of bright yellow stickers that said things like "Queer" and "Hella Gay." Everyone took a few and stuck them to their clothes, unconcerned with which ones they wore and what it meant to do so. (Many of them were straight and just liked free stickers.) I stuck one of each on my chest, thrilled at having all these new terms to apply to myself.

That night I drank too much and danced too sloppily, but I was happy. Being in such an explicitly queer space lifted a weight off my shoulders I hadn't even known was there. The relatively few crushes I'd had on other women before that night had always felt unserious, or winky—the way women's magazines talk about their readers' collective "girl crush" on the newest, prettiest famous twenty-year-old. But being at that party, surrounded by girls who were dancing together and flirting with one another and kissing, I felt empowered to take my queerness seriously. I could look at women not just as the kind of people I made friends with but as the kind of people I might one day love. My sexuality—however "late" it had come to me, however it had shifted (and might shift again)—was real, and worthy. It was okay that I didn't have a word for it, or a story that made sense to other people. I gave myself permission to meet my heart where it was.

Like so much else, this was easier decided than done. When I went to the Pride parade the next day, I felt uncomfortable taking a spot on my company's float alongside the people I thought of as "actually" queer: the Out ones, the ones who always knew, the ones who knew what it felt like to have their hearts broken by unrequited love for their middle school best friends. So I walked alongside them, searching the crowd for something that might make everything clear. I wanted people to see me, believe me. Maybe I wanted someone to yell something at us, or hold up some sign for us, that would convince me of my belonging by grouping us together. I wanted assurance that nobody else thought of me as an impostor, even if I still felt like one, even as I knew there wasn't anyone out there who could do that for me but me.

When I'd walked for about an hour—much of it in the rain, hungover, and after a four-hour delay on our float's start time—I snuck away from the pack, weaving as quickly as I could through the hundreds of people pressed against the barricades. As I always do when escaping a crowded event and/or social situation, I immediately felt one hundred times better. I was happy to have been there, but I was even happier to be on my way home, where everything had stayed the same.

I don't know how paranoid I'm being (I have to assume it's at least a little), but I get this sense that when I talk to straight women about guys now, my opinion matters less than it did when I was one of them. How much of that is owed to the fact that I am not single and how much is owed to the fact that I am dating a woman, I don't know. Some of it, surely, is that I find myself less interested in hearing about men, and presumably my friends can tell. There is a particular kind of commiseration done between women who date men, and for so much of my life, it was my favorite thing to do. Anytime I met a woman who had a crush on a guy, I wanted to know everything about it: the backstory, the eye contact, the signs, the texts. I have had this conversation with women I worked with at the writing center where I tutored in college, with women I met drunk in frat-house bathrooms, with women I bought coffee from, and pretty much every girl I ever sat next to, in front of, or behind in every high school class and college class I've ever taken. I have been the friend that other girls refer their friends to when they are tired of hearing about a boy and need someone else to fill in for a while. I don't think this is necessarily because I ever had anything especially insightful to say, and it certainly wasn't because I understood men or how to ensnare them. I was just eager, and wanted to hear every last detail. Not everyone wants the exact timeline, spelling, and punctuation of the text conversation you had with the boy you like, but I do. Or at least, I did.

When I came out I assumed I would continue to relate to my existing friends the way I always had. I hoped I would make new friends, queer ones, whom I could relate to in another way, but it did not occur to me that the dynamics between me and my straight friends would change. Boys made up a lot (probably too much) of what we'd talked about over the years, but there was so much I hadn't even experienced yet. Now that I was actually in a relationship, there was a brand-new world of neuroses I needed to process, repeatedly, with as many friends as would listen.

But it did not take me long to figure out that asking friends for relationship advice is a very mixed bag, and that I'd been overconfident and overeager in dispersing so much of it over the years. I learned that fraught text exchanges with someone who is ambivalent about you at best can make for great, dishy happy-hour conversations, but recapping the pleasantly domestic weekend you had with your steady girlfriend does not. I'd rather the latter over the former, hands down, but there is something sad in unclenching your fist around that specific kind of agony. I hated feeling fed up and frustrated and unsure if the person I liked would ever like me back, but I miss the blind support that came along with it. How tender toward me, and how brutal on my behalf, were my friends when a man let me down.

But now I have no men to speak of. It used to be that I'd meet up with a writer friend of mine for brunch every three or so months, and each time she would ask about the guy I'd hopefully told her about last time. Then I would spend half an hour recounting everything that went wrong since I saw her last, and she'd perform outrage, stabbing her fork into brioche French toast and suggesting I get my revenge by dating four guys at once. We did not know a lot about each other, but she always remembered the names of the guys I liked, and she always made me feel so much better when it turned out they did not like me. The last time I saw her she was weeks away from her wedding, and I had just started dating Lydia. We were so happy for each other. We talked for just an hour. For months I kept meaning to email her, to set up another brunch, but it's been over a year since then, and I suspect we've lost the rhythm.

It is a good sign, I know, not having a lot of drama or insecurity to contend with in a relationship. I suppose it's a good thing that I don't need as much support from as many friends as I used to, and my friends are probably relieved to no longer have to give so much of it. But I miss them. I am mostly very content and I am confident that the person I love loves me. I am also a little lonely, in a way I did not expect. The thing I used to talk about most, and bond over most, is all but gone, and I haven't been able to figure out how to replace it.

In the summer of 2016 I went to New York City's Pride March for the first (and maybe last?) time as an officially out gay person. This time I didn't march with my job; I don't actually recall being given the option. Either way, I didn't want to. I wanted to attend as a spectator, and I wanted to go with my newish gay friends. A few months earlier, Lydia's best friend (and, as it happens, first high school girlfriend) Jenna and Jenna's then-girlfriend Caitlin followed her example and moved across the country from San Diego to Brooklyn. I was both nervous and excited for them to arrive, knowing even as I was doing it that I was placing all my best-lesbian-couple-friends hopes and dreams on two women I'd never met. Up until Pride we hadn't actually seen them a whole lot—not for any major reason other than an accumulation of tiny misalignments between who we were and what we liked to do when we were not at work. Pride, though, was something we could agree on.

Two weeks earlier, a racist and homophobic security guard named Omar Mateen had murdered forty-nine people and injured fifty-three others inside Pulse, a gay club in Orlando, Florida. Pulse was hosting Latin Night, which was likely a major factor in Mateen's timing. Most of the victims were Latinx, and many of them were immigrants. The shooting was the deadliest act of violence against queer people in U.S. history, and the deadliest terrorist attack here, period, since 9/11.

I do not often feel singled out by hatred in this country. I am white and comfortably middle-class. Many people hate women, but I guess I am used to all the ways that particular venom flows through my daily life. Before the Orlando shooting, anti-LGBTQ violence was something that happened to other people. It was devastating but it was not personal. I was not at risk for that particular form of bigotry. I am still much safer than most. Still, Orlando created a possibility I had never before considered for myself.

So it seemed extra-important, that year, to be at Pride. And I wanted to be around all the people who understood why.

Also attending with us was another queer couple we knew from our Brooklyn neighborhood. One of the pair, Sellers, was, like me, in her first-ever same-sex relationship, and it would be her first Pride as a queer woman, too. So I suppose I imagined the six of us going there together and experiencing some kind of rainbow-heavy communal gay transcendence. No matter if we weren't all that close when we left for the parade; when we got back from it, we would be inseparable.

Suffice it to say, I did what I always do before a big event or holiday: set myself up for disappointment.

First of all, we were late. I'd been made to "play it by ear," which in my experience means that several things will go wrong and I won't be allowed to get mad about it. By the time the six of us actually found one another along the parade route, the last handful of floats were making their way down Christopher Street. We wound through the crowd, getting as close as we could to the metal railings without touching the backs of the people in front of us. If I stood on my tiptoes I could just barely make out

Samira Wiley and Natasha Lyonne and Dascha Polanco walking beneath the *Orange Is the New Black* float. Feeling claustrophobic and completely unable to hear one another speak, we agreed by hand gesture to make our way over to PrideFest.

PrideFest had been described to me as a "gay street fair" with art and shopping and free food. Which sounded great. The reality was much closer to a student-orientation fair at a college campus, only instead of signing up to join ten clubs whose meetings you'd never attend, you could sign up to receive brand emails. We walked down the street, lined on either side with plastic-covered booths and awnings, and every time I passed one for a life-insurance company or a granola-bar company I assumed I was getting closer to the real PrideFest. Up front, maybe, it was all marketing, but there was supposed to be more. Who had told me there would be art? Who had told me that any of this would be queer? Truly, the only thing separating the Fest from every other fair I've attended in a high school gym was that the brands were pandering to gay people instead of just young ones. Mostly this meant that their banners and T-shirts had rainbows on them. Some companies fit in more successfully than others, and ultimately I'd rather buy from a brand that is at least willing to align itself with gay people than refuse them outright, but walking down that street I felt repulsed, not proud. And I am no righteous consumer. I buy things off Amazon all the time. I have little to no ground to stand on as far as any rejection of capitalism goes. I still don't know exactly what I'd expected or hoped for. I just know it wasn't that.

After we reached the end of the stalls, the six of us split up into our three respective couples, despite my dreams of instant best-friendship. Each pair of us was vaguely annoyed with the way the others were handling the parade's crowds. I was mildly devastated. On our walk to the subway, Lydia and I sat on someone's steps to complain. And then—feeling helpless as to what to do or think or feel about Orlando now that the media had mostly moved on, hating that an event ostensibly created to celebrate and to heal felt so empty and so crassly commercial, upset with myself for having expected a parade to be life-changing and for ending up annoyed with everyone I went with instead—I cried. Here was the one day a year specifically dedicated to queer community and celebration, and there we were, alone, together, wondering what to do now. That I had Lydia there with me was no minor source of happiness and relief, but I wanted so much more.

Not very long after we'd stopped, a group of women walked by us holding Solo cups and singing. When they saw us they said hi, and rather generously asked if we wanted some of their pot. When we demurred they asked if they could take a selfie with us, so we did. I never saw the photo, and I can only hope it wasn't too obvious that I had been crying. That was the best part of the whole day for me: seeing and being seen by other queer women, huddling together and smiling because it was our special day, and we had that one thing in common.

14

WOMEN'S STUDIES 101

Lydia often points other people's gawking out to me, a tendency which, early on in our relationship, usually made me roll my eyes. She would come home from work and tell me about a customer who stared at her a beat too long while paying for her coffee, and I would groan, thinking she wanted me to be jealous. Or we'd be walking to our favorite sushi place for dinner, and she would pull gently on my arm and ask, "Did you hear those guys laughing at us?" I never noticed it myself, and so I assumed she was imagining things. "Not everyone is always looking at you," I'd tell her. We live in Brooklyn, in a neighborhood that, to me, seems dense with queer women. It isn't at all uncommon to see a pair of women holding hands as they walk down the sidewalk; I know because my eyes are drawn to them like moths to a big, gay flame. I knew there were many places in the world in which we'd stand out, but Brooklyn (and New York City at large) wasn't one of them.

I don't know why, exactly, I was so eager to disbelieve her. If anyone who wasn't my own girlfriend had been the one telling me that someone had treated them differently for being queer, I would have believed them without reservation. Or maybe I just want to think I would. How could it happen as much as Lydia said it did when half the time I was right next to her and I never saw anything? Maybe it just seemed impossible that it could happen— was happening, consistently—to someone I lived with and loved. And if it could happen to someone this close to me, then maybe it could happen to me, too.

I sometimes feel a sort of lingering guilt about how relatively easy it was for me to come out. It's totally unproductive, and self-involved, and perhaps a little masochistic to spend any time thinking about how I should have had to suffer more for my sexuality, but I can't help it. It's not that I think I deserve to be discriminated against; it's that I don't think anyone does, and it doesn't seem fair that I should have weathered my coming-out as smoothly as I did.

After I came out to everyone I knew (and later to everyone I didn't), I went about my life paying very little attention to how people responded to my relationship. I am a little spacey to begin with, often walking by people I know without realizing because I am looking at the pavement, absorbed in my thoughts. But it also took me a while to get used to the idea that I was no longer presumed normal. The little things caught up to me: At night, in unfamiliar neighborhoods, I would instinctively keep my hand thrust inside my pocket when I might otherwise reach for my girlfriend's hand. I learned to distinguish a curious glance from a disapproving one. A couple of summers ago I booked a cabin for Lydia and me over the phone, and I reflexively referred to her as "my friend." When we arrived for check-in months later, the skittish, off-put reaction of the cabin's middle-aged female manager to Lydia's appearance—androgynous, makeup-less, the sides of her head shaved—seemed to confirm that I had been right to be cautious. But then I wondered if I was just being paranoid. Back in the car, I asked Lydia if she thought the manager had looked at us weird.

"Of course she did," she said. "Look at me."

As soon as Lydia was old enough to talk, she began to protest her clothes. There is a picture of her—my favorite picture of her—at four years old, wearing a frilly dress at her uncle's wedding. She looks desperately unhappy; her mouth is a perfect, upside-down semicircle. Eventually her mother gave in to her requests and let her wear what she wanted. Around that same time, her mom received an anonymous letter from a self-described "concerned mother," presumably of one of Lydia's preschool peers, advising her that if she continued to let her little girl wear boys' clothes, she would end up a lesbian. She threw it away and let Lydia wear what she wanted, which I am grateful for, especially because of the pictures.

I know what Lydia's favorite childhood outfit was because she has described it to me at least seven times: a pair of what she calls *"Beetlejuice* pants" worn with a white button-up shirt, a black vest and cummerbund, and a top hat. At six years old she had her hair cut short and slicked it back with water in order to look more like her idol, Zack Morris. When she was in kindergarten, a group of eighth grade girls told her she was in the wrong bathroom, and after that she was so afraid to go into public women's bathrooms that she'd hold it as long as she possibly could, and once peed her pants in a bathroom stall because she hadn't gotten there quite quickly enough. She still hates public restrooms. On a trip to Paris, at the Musée de l'Armée, a guard called out to stop her from going into the women's bathroom with me. I don't speak French, but I knew enough to know he was asking if she was a man or a woman. "Femme!" I hissed, and if I'd known how I would have also said: *and mind your own fucking business.* Lydia was annoyed, but she was also used to it.

Once, she and I were sitting on the subway holding hands when a group of Russian-speaking tourists (two men and two women) got on a few stops after ours. As usual, I didn't pay them much attention beyond registering their foreign language and exuberant tourist-ness. I was thinking only of lunch. We got off the train at Fourteenth Street, and once we were safely out of earshot she said, "They were talking about us."

"Who?" I said.

"The Russians."

"How do you know?" I asked. I knew the answer—Lydia took two years of Russian in college—but sometimes in a relationship it's nice to needlessly challenge your partner's expertise on something they like to brag about, like knowing how to speak a little Russian.

"They said 'lesbians' and 'girls' and 'illegal,'" said Lydia. "And they wouldn't sit by us."

"Really?" I asked.

"Yes."

"Maybe they said, 'Those girls make a beautiful lesbian couple, and it's truly a shame that homosexuality is illegal in our country,'" I offered, optimistically. If I teased her, if I made a joke, I thought, maybe it would hurt less. I don't know.

"I don't think so," said Lydia, and I didn't really think so, either.

When I was a senior in high school, my civics teacher assigned me to argue against legalizing gay marriage in a mock debate. We were working our way through the typical high school civics class debate topics—the war in Iraq, torture, capital punishment, welfare, abortion, and, finally, gay marriage—and though he did not say so explicitly, my suspicion was that my teacher was assigning students to argue against the positions he assumed they held. Or else it was just a coincidence that all of the popular kids in the class—Young Life Christians, every last one—were made to argue for abortion rights and against the death penalty. I'm sure the intent was to make us learn a little something about the other side and come out of class a little wiser for it, but like so many other high school team projects, it mostly served to strengthen the inalienable supremacy of the popular kids. There were more of them in that classroom than there were of the rest of us, and somehow they were all friends, which in turn made it harder to debate them. Even the dumb ones.

So there were two reasons I didn't want to argue against legalizing same-sex marriage: one, because I hate losing, and two, because I was very much in favor of equal marriage rights. So much so, in fact, that when I received my assignment, I went to my teacher after class to ask if I could possibly switch sides. I do not remember crying, but after a later parent-teacher conference, my parents told me my teacher had said I cried. (And if I did, why not keep that between us, Mr. H? My parents did not need more evidence of my uncoolness.) My teacher was sympathetic, but he did not let me switch teams, which was the correct teacher move to make. To prepare for my debate I printed off a bunch of excerpts from Christian philosophy papers and the Bible and old-school psychologists who argued that for a child to grow up healthy, he needed to be raised by one woman and one man. My team won, which was obviously bittersweet.

For most of my life, my politics revolved around what I perceived to be the issues I faced as a woman. Toward the end of high school, I got into politics, and more specifically, a very introductory, very second-wave, very white kind of feminism. Although heading into college as a freshman my extracurriculars were limited to friends, boys, drinking (and the drama that ensued as a result of all three), as a sophomore, and a newly declared political science major, I saw a flyer for a Feminist Majority Leadership Alliance meeting and decided I should—as our career counselors liked to say—"get involved." At the very first meeting I went to, the current president announced there would be elections for new leadership the following week, because she and the vice president were both seniors and wanted the transition of power over our six-member club to be as painless as possible. So with one whole meeting under my belt, I decided I wanted to be the group's next president. My campaign was a thirty-second speech about my interest and my organizational ability. My opponent was a junior who seemed like the kind of person who would miss half the meetings for eccentric spiritual reasons, so I won. I'd persuaded my roommate Joyce to join my platform as vice president by insisting it would be good for her eventual medical school application, and promising I would basically do all the work myself, a move I now recognize as somewhat despotic. Our new treasurer ran reluctantly, and unopposed.

Being Feminist President gave me a sense of purpose and identity like I'd never experienced before. There was a brief period in middle school when I was the Spelling Bee Kid, but I was neither the only nor the best one, so it didn't really count. I'd never felt like part of a team before, really, either—my athletic record revealed a string of sports I tried for one season before quitting as soon as I realized I'd never be a star. I quit clarinet, D.A.R.E., yearbook, and Spanish Club. Eventually I had tennis to count on, but I never got great, and as far as team bonding and social clout go, tennis isn't exactly basketball or soccer.

I relished being a part of something bigger, and unsurprisingly, I found it delightful to be in charge. I loved emailing discussion topics and relevant articles to our

Listserv the day before our meetings, and then feeling in-
dignant when attendance was poor, or nobody had much
to say—both of which happened often. I loved coordinat-
ing with the business office and the school events planner
and local companies to organize our annual women's
health fair, like a grown-up with an actual job. I loved
walking around campus with Joyce in the evenings to
tape up posters. And I really loved writing angry letters to
the editor of our school's terrible student newspaper when
they published something sexist, typing, under my name:
President, FMLA.

I ran all the same second-waver events my predecessor
before me had run: the Equal Pay Bake Sale, the Take
Back the Night marches, the *Vagina Monologues* performances, the "Love Your Body" campaigns. All the usual
Feminism 101 fare—all of it important and well-meant
and valid enough, very little of it as universally pressing or
as progressive as I considered it then. (Though even this
entry-level feminism was too much for plenty of people,
and how I loved the righteous outrage I felt when I saw
one of our handmade posters defaced, or when a male
student stopped by the bake sale to tell me the wage gap
was fake.) Our most daring and most poorly attended
event was the joint pro-choice march we held with Illinois
State, which has an enrollment of about twenty thousand.
Maybe twenty people showed up, which was fine, because
my vice president and I were profoundly hungover, having
scheduled the march for the Sunday after all the fraterni-
ties held their Halloween parties.

· · ·

Being *the* outspoken feminist on campus also gave me another reason why I never seemed to get anywhere with guys, and I was always looking for more of those. I don't know what it's like on college campuses now, but in 2007, the only thing straight boys wanted less to do with than the campus feminist club was the gay-straight alliance. During "Love Your Body" Week I sat outside the cafeteria at a folding table during lunch, trying to get people to circle their favorite body part on a piece of paper featuring the generic outline of a human body, which I'd printed three hundred of in the library. It was hard enough getting anyone to stop when food was so near, and then the crowds of frat boys would pour in through the doors, smirking when they saw the big FMLA sign. Occasionally one of them would come over to circle a crotch. On the second or third day of this I saw my sort-of-friend Eric, a senior who played for the men's tennis team and who'd kissed me once at a party. When he saw me he said "Katie! You're a feminist?" in the same sort of tone you might use to ask someone if they are currently picking their nose. I saw myself in that instant as Alice Paul, or Margaret Sanger, or any of the other historical white women I was learning about in my Women's Studies 101 class. My chest puffed up, and I jutted out my chin, and I said, "Yes. I. Am."

Because most of the boys I went to school with were so visibly turned off by even the word "feminism," and because feminism was my thing, it felt a little less hurtful and a little more righteous when we didn't get along. It wasn't that I didn't like guys, period. I just didn't like guys who were sexist, and as far as I could tell, that was most of them. And it wasn't that guys didn't like me because they could tell I didn't like them—they didn't like me because I was a proud feminist, and that scared them. (The best thing a friend or magazine can give you when you are a single straight woman is the idea that you are single because you're "intimidating." Honestly, what could be more flattering?) The older I got, and the more men I met, the less I liked them; and the less I liked them, the easier it was to think of them as this one big, bad thing. It's not like it's particularly hard to find evidence if your working hypothesis is that all men are bad. One must simply go online.

But in mistaking my own discomfort with dating men for some sort of political enlightenment, my feminism got whittled down into something myopic and powerless. I reveled in self-pity. I made it too simple: men bad, women good.

It used to be so easy to feel right, which has to be one of the main perks of being twenty-two. It was at that age that I got an equal sign—for feminism, specifically—tattooed on the inside of my right wrist. Not since then have I been remotely as sure that my side of any argument is the right one. Not since then have I believed that most people agree on essential human rights and values, and all they need to see that is a good, clear presentation of the facts. By the time I finished my public policy graduate program I felt disheartened and depressed by what I had learned—mainly: that people rarely change their minds (and when they do, it's to get more conservative as they age), that you should never take a poll or a politician's word at face value, and that getting the government to do much of anything good takes decades. The starry-eyed political fervor with which I'd ridden in a van full of College Democrats to Indiana to canvass for Barack Obama had been all but drained from my body by the time I graduated. At the time, I resented policy school for making me lose my faith in government. Now I wonder if that was kind of the point, and maybe everyone should have to go.

The Supreme Court ruled in favor of federally recognized same-sex marriage the summer I came out, about ten years after I'd argued against it in civics class. And that victory matters, a lot. But I wonder if in a hundred years we will treat 2015 as the year everything changed for all American queer people the way we treat 1920 as the year everything changed for all American women. When my mostly white women's studies classmates and I talked about suffrage, we marveled over the fact that "we" had gained the right to vote only ninety years earlier—never mind that women and men of color were frequently disenfranchised until the Voting Rights Act was ratified in 1965, and ignoring that voter suppression still happens today. The Equal Pay Bake Sales I helped organize charged men a dollar per cookie and women seventy-five cents—never mind that that ratio described white wage earners only. And yet I was so sure we were radical, and seeing things so much more clearly than everyone else.

Maybe the law that makes it legal for me to marry my girlfriend seems less like the paradigm-shifting legislation I thought it was at eighteen because now I'm thirty, and that law actually applies to my life, and I can see that it hasn't made everything fair. Under the Trump administration, it feels low on the list of urgent concerns. But maybe I'll regret my lack of fear for myself two years from now; if Trump's election taught me anything, it's that things can always get worse than you imagine. I have to remind myself that there are people out there, lots of them, who find me inferior and immoral. That I am still able to be surprised by intolerance and hatred is a function of how privileged I have been. I'm a white, middle-class, cisgendered woman who came out as an adult living in New York City during the Obama administration. I took it for granted that my rights as a woman and a newly out queer person were the safest they'd ever been and would only continue to get safer. I was so sure that Hillary Clinton would win the election that I served for a while as on-demand reassurance to my more worried friends. Chiara would text me a screenshot of an unfavorable new poll, and I would text back: Polls don't mean anything, trust me.

Well.

I don't know much of anything, but I know more than I did ten years ago, when I thought I knew everything. And while I had a lot of fun believing I knew everything, I would have been better off if I'd given it up sooner. Perhaps I could have done more with my little feminist administration than awareness campaigns and bake sales. Because feminism is—has to be—about more than loving our bodies and empowering our sexuality and celebrating badass white ladies throughout history. I am embarrassed I subscribed to that version of feminism for as long as I did. I am embarrassed I once considered marriage equality the civil rights movement of our time when the black civil rights struggle was—and is—very much ongoing. When I experience sexism, I experience it as a white woman. When I experience anti-queer prejudice, I experience it as a cisgendered gay woman living in a big, progressive city. My perspective is limited. There is so much I do not know.

The day after President Trump was inaugurated, I went to the Women's March in Manhattan, and as I walked I watched the teenagers and college kids. Their signs—and their face paint and outfits—were unquestionably superior to everyone else's, in design and humor and inclusive messaging alike, and their chants were the catchiest, and loudest. It was a great day, beautiful and uplifting and invigorating after a couple of months' worth of disbelief and despair. It wasn't perfect, and it wasn't enough, in itself, to change things. It was still very early, and Trump hadn't had enough time to do much yet. But it was heartening. And when the president does something despicable—and he finds a way most days—and I feel overcome by my weird useless helplessness and my grown-up cynicism, I try to think instead of the many young people I saw at the March: proudly queer and black and Latinx and immigrant and feminist, already so aware of just how much those things can mean.

15

ROOMMATES

I have never in my life wanted an apartment to myself. Maybe it would have been different had I been forced to go the Craigslist route, but for ten years, I lived with best friends. When I started thinking I might want to move to New York, there was only one potential roommate in my mind: Chiara. Ours is the easiest, most seamless transition from strangers to friends that I have ever made. As roommates we were companionable if not inseparable, like Rylee and I had been. We watched the *Today* show together in the mornings before going to work, and one or two nights a week ordered heaps of buttery pasta and bread from our favorite delivery place, and ate it on TV trays in our seventy-square-foot "living room." She was not around as often as I was, but she was there when it counted. When I was dumped by the man I'd briefly dated shortly after moving to New York, Chiara made me get out of bed and go on a ghost tour of the historical home museum where she volunteered as a guide, because it was almost Halloween. I stood in the back of the group, the guides playing clips from recordings taken by ghost hunters, and tried not to cry. Then we rented *Bridget Jones's Diary* from a combination pizza place/video rental shop in the East Village. When Chiara broke up with a boyfriend I hated, we watched Eurovision on her laptop in her bed for two days straight.

When we first moved in together, everyone, including us, thought it was funny that I'd written a book about how bad I was at dating, and Chiara had written an actual guidebook on it called *Modern Dating: A Field Guide.* This dynamic was omnipresent in our relationship as friends and roommates. I asked for boy advice, and she gave it. I complained about my bad dating luck, and she told me I needed to put myself out there more. I went on dating apps largely because I felt I had to prove to her that I was trying. I dated a little, but not so much that it ever really took me away from her. She was single for the first five months we lived together, but even then it felt like she knew something I didn't. Then she got a boyfriend and I was sure of it. That boyfriend, beyond being annoying in a more general sense, was also fairly hot and cold with Chiara, and so she was still around a fair amount, even if she would have preferred to be with him. When he was busy with work or otherwise engaged, we stayed in and watched reality TV, and the only real difference was that she kept her phone in her hand.

But they broke up, and a month later Chiara met Mark, and it was clear very early on that this relationship was going to be different. They had their literal third date in Italy. She was going to visit family, and made a joke about him coming to visit, and then he bought a plane ticket. He proposed while they were there. (She said no, not yet.) I was briefly aghast, until I met him. Right away I liked him, and I liked them together. So when she started hanging out with him every night (and, unsurprisingly, that happened pretty quickly), it was a little easier to bear than if it had been a guy I liked less. But only a little.

When I complained to friends that Chiara had abandoned me, and left me the apartment to myself, they told me I had it made. I disagreed. When Chiara really lived with me, there was a chance that I would end up doing something with my day that I had not been planning to do from the moment I woke up. Without her, there was nobody around to pull me out of the routine I'd made for myself. I was never going to be surprised to find, after walking up the five flights of stairs to our apartment, that the lights were on and she was home.

I'm making it sound like Chiara died. Mark's apartment was twenty blocks away. They invited me to things. He tried hard, especially relative to other boyfriends I've known. For a while they made a point of staying at our place a few nights a week. Then she'd just come by on Sundays, to hang out with me and swap out her dirty clothes for clean ones. We'd order pasta and watch an old musical, and in the morning, she would go home. Then, over the holidays they went to Peru together for ten days, and after that she didn't come back. It had gotten too hard to pretend like what was obviously happening wasn't happening. She lived with someone else. And despite my best efforts, I lived alone. I hated every second.

So three months later, and four months before the Manhattan lease I shared with Chiara was up, I moved to Brooklyn. She and I found a pair of subletters, and I signed a new lease on a beautiful apartment that felt, comparatively speaking, like a mansion. I was living with my good friend Rachel, and I was excited not only because I loved her, and loved our new apartment, but because, like me, she had never dated anyone. Finally, I thought, I am living with a kindred spirit. I didn't have to worry about her abandoning me halfway into the year. Especially not when our apartment was so pretty.

It did not for a second occur to me that I would be the one to disrupt the dynamic of our roommate-ship in its infancy. But that is exactly what happened. Rachel and I moved into our new apartment together on April 1. Just over three months later, I met Lydia. It did not take very long for Lydia and I to start hanging out every day. In the first month or so we'd grant each other the pretense that we had other things going on, suggesting future dates three or four nights after the one we were on as if it were the next time we'd both be free. But you can keep up the illusion of a wide-ranging social life for only so long when you are texting the same person every day and night. Once we started regularly sleeping over at each other's apartments (conveniently, we happened to live exactly one and a half blocks apart), the jig was up. When either of us asked the other in the morning if she had plans for that night, we told the truth: no, not yet, not unless it's hanging out with you.

In the first five or six months, I tried to respect Rachel—and by extension, my former self—by making sure Lydia and I slept over at her apartment as many nights as we slept over at mine. The problem was that we agreed: my apartment was much nicer, and quieter, and closer (even by just a block and a half) to Lydia's job. So then we just started shooting for two or three nights a week at her place. I never didn't feel guilty when I opened my front door with Lydia behind me and found Rachel at home. She didn't even mind, which almost made it worse. In her position I had often been so much less forgiving.

When Lydia moved into Rachel's and my apartment, about ten months into our relationship, it mostly formalized something that was already true. Because our apartment is big and because Lydia essentially lived there anyway, it made sense to make it official. We'd known it was coming for a while, I think, but had held out until the practicality of it safely overruled our respective neuroses: hers (developed after an ex kicked her out after just three weeks of living together), that moving into someone else's apartment is a relationship's death knell; mine, that moving in together before it's been a year is the same. It wasn't that either of us stopped worrying about these things, exactly, but that we wanted to live together more than we wanted to avoid the potential consequences of it. Lydia found a subletter, and we spent a day hauling her belongings from her place to mine—or, as I had to get in the habit of calling it, ours.

Even before we lived together, I found myself rushing to get home—from work, from the gym, from drinks with a friend—so I could meet up with Lydia. And I am an extremely fast walker. Once, in high school, my friend Tara's boyfriend said he'd seen me somewhere in town but hadn't said hi to me because I was "hauling ass." But that is just my normal walking speed. I hate being in transit; I just want to be there. And usually, there is home. I have never in my life been the last one at a party. The last time I excelled in hangout duration was in high school, the era of sleepovers. Then, my eyes weren't dragged to the clock, calculating what time I'd get home if I left right then. I was stuck there, forced to enjoy myself until morning. So long as I have somewhere else to be and something else to do before I climb into bed that night, it is very hard for me to relax. This is all to say: I rushed home in the days before I met Lydia, too. But with her there, I rushed home even sooner. Sometimes, I would find myself half-running to the subway, or up to my front door. If she had other plans that was one thing, but it was hard for me to be out knowing that she was home and I was not. Even still I sometimes act as though we have a fixed allotment of days together, and I do not want to be responsible for selling us short.

Mostly what I think this means is that I am in love.

But how bad, exactly, should I feel for choosing my significant other over my friends? I am certain it's at least a little. Here I must offer a mea culpa for all the times I've said or implied that I would never do that. I retract each instance of single-person sanctimony, and I acknowledge here and now that I did not know what I was talking about when I said I would do friendship differently in a relationship than it had been done to me. I think and I hope that I am still a good friend, but I am not the same friend that I was when I was single. I choose Lydia over friends all the time.

I feel bad when I leave parties early or tell a friend I can't hang out for no good reason other than wanting to hang out with my girlfriend instead. Usually, I still do it anyway. I go back and forth constantly between thinking I am getting steadily worse as a person and thinking that this is just what happens when you get older. (Worse yet: that both things are true.) You get into a relationship, you move in together, you stay in more and go to bed earlier, and your world gets smaller. Having been the person who must be fit into someone else's schedule, given a slot before the boyfriend gets home or on a night he is away, I should have seen it coming. But I did not expect to be part of the problem. I expected my friends to grow flakey and distant when they were in relationships, but not me. I spent so much of my life feeling like I kept my friendships thanks in large part to the strength of my grip; I did not expect that I might one day choose to let go.

But I have a girlfriend now, and my friendships are not in place. I have loosened my grip, and not even totally against my will. Falling in love and being in a relationship with someone who is always there has taught me that I don't need my friends as urgently and desperately as I sometimes did when I was younger and alone, and afraid I always would be. I still don't know whether that's a good thing. I just know that when I find myself thinking about calling a friend or asking her to hang out and then decide not to, I feel awful, every time.

And yet I feel more secure in the degree to which I am loved than I ever have before. Lydia and I cook for each other, watch shows together, go to sleep and wake up together. We don't do a whole lot with other people, and half the time, when we do, we end up wishing we'd just hung out alone, together. I am living with the best roommate I have ever had.

I met Chiara for a drink a week before she got married. I wasn't going to be at the wedding, which had been a source of some tension between us, and some not inconsiderable guilt on my part. The wedding, fittingly, would be in Italy. I did not go for several reasons, some of them better than others: I didn't think I could afford it and I knew that Lydia couldn't; my brother was getting married just a month later and I'd have to travel for that; the wedding involved a Catholic mass and I wanted nothing to do with a church that said my own relationship was wrong. Weddings in general make me squeamish, though that isn't and wasn't considered a good enough reason in itself not to go. I do not like much about wedding tradition, and having to listen to friends talk about battling in-laws over table settings makes me want to cut off my own head. But that's not a popular opinion, especially not among brides-to-be. It was very difficult for me to be empathetic and kind when Chiara talked to me about her wedding, and I am not proud of it. At the bar, we sat on the patio, shielding our eyes from the sun and sort of dancing around the topics common to someone in the lead-up to their wedding. But it was clear to me that Chiara was restraining herself, and it was probably clear to her that I didn't really want any more detail than she was giving me.

Up until I saw her off, I felt secure in my decision not to go. She had been mostly gracious about it, and only a little resentful—particularly when I ended up buying plane tickets to Paris for ten days, two months after her wedding, for not all that much less than it would have cost me to get to Italy. We both knew it wasn't an exact exchange, but still, it made my choice feel that much more deliberate. Our importance to each other had changed. First because of Mark, and then because of Lydia, and then because of—I don't know what. Many little things that had slowly and then quickly caught up with us. When we got up to leave the bar I wished her well, and hugged her, and we talked about how funny it was that when I saw her next, she'd be married.

I regretted not going to Chiara's wedding as soon as I saw the first picture of her in Italy on Instagram. She is standing in front of the church where she will be married, which is the same church her grandparents married in. She looks pretty and relaxed.

She is not relaxed. A few days into the trip (she flew out a week before the ceremony), she sends me a Chiara-esque string of texts. She says something like:

Hmmmm
I'm curious to see
Like
If I'm going to feel . . .

The euphoria? That all my married friends say is coming?
Because I get married in two days and
I've never felt more stressed in my life.

I am surprised because every one of the pictures I've
seen so far has made her look both euphoric and un-
stressed. I feel comforted, too, because high-stakes, high-
pressure events make me miserable, and I am all but
positive that my own eventual wedding day, should I have
one, will be very far from the most magical day of my life.
I am relieved: even though she is days away from getting
married, she is still my friend, harried and funny and particular. I am relieved that I am still the person she wants
to vent to, even though I am not there. I hope for her that
her wedding day is exactly what she wants, and I don't
want her to come home feeling unhappy with how it all
went. But hearing how stressed she is makes me feel a bit
smug. I am right to feel as negatively about weddings as I
do, I think. I was right not to go.

On the Saturday that Chiara got married, I woke up
at home. I grabbed my phone and opened Instagram, realizing their afternoon ceremony was likely under way.
There was nothing posted yet, so I carried my phone with
me around the apartment as I brushed my teeth, ate
breakfast, put on makeup, refreshing her wedding hash-
tag every five minutes. Finally, I saw one: a photo of Chiara and Mark emerging from the old church, radiant, rice
falling all around them. She looked so beautiful, and so
happy.

I should have been there.

So this is why you go to your friends' weddings, even

if they are expensive, and stressful, and far away—to see them this happy. To just see them, period. For a long time after Chiara moved out I assumed we'd eventually resume some sort of weekly routine, thinking we'd find a way to make it easy and natural for us both. In other words, I was being lazy. It wasn't going to get any easier. For that reason alone, I should have gone.

The next day, Chiara replied to my texted congratulations, and told me it had happened: she'd been euphoric, and the wedding was perfect. The best day of her life. My friend had not lost out on a perfect day by my not being at her wedding, but I might have.

Girl #6

. . . .

Marissa Cooper, ages sixteen to nineteen. When I watched *The O.C.* for the first time, I had a crush on Seth just like everybody else. He was cute, he was funny, he ad-libbed his lines, et cetera. Marissa, on the other hand, was who I wanted to be. I wanted every ridiculous outfit, and I wanted that little side-bang she had that seemed to operate outside the laws of gravity. She was the most beautiful person I had ever seen on television, all sharp edges and melancholy deep-blue eyes. In the brief, sweeps-centric period in which she dated Alex, the gorgeous punk with the purple streaks in her hair played by Olivia Wilde, I was annoyed (I knew ratings desperation when I saw it), but I was also transfixed. All my friends hated Marissa, and I got it, and still do—she was needlessly dramatic, careless, and flighty, a poor little rich girl created by writers to experience way too much way too quickly. But I rooted for her anyway. And when she died in the season-three finale—an episode I'd had to record and watch on VHS tape hours later—and the credits played, I rolled onto my stomach on the floor of my basement and sobbed.

16

HOSPITAL CORNERS

have made my bed every day of my life since I was first told to make my bed, which I have to believe happened as soon as I was tall enough to clear the top of it. There are chores my mother needed to remind me to do (dusting, primarily, which to my mind is a battle so losing it isn't worth being waged), but unlike for my younger brothers, making my bed was never among them. It makes inherent sense to me as a daily restoration of order. Compared to other chores, it's low in labor, high in emotional and mental reward. It's the yoga class of housework.

Never was my perpetual, stringent bed-making an issue for anyone until I got into a relationship. My bed was mine and mine alone. In college, maybe, I occasionally thought of making my bed as an act of preparation—

the possibility of my bringing someone back to my room
at the end of the night at least existed, however faintly—
but even then, I had a twin bed. Nobody ever saw it but
my roommates, and they couldn't have cared less what I
did with it. (Not that a guy would have, either; on the few
occasions I went home with men as an adult, their beds
were always profoundly unmade, and one would hope
they wouldn't have had a double standard about it.) The
argument against bed-making as a person who lives and
sleeps alone is always that there's no one to impress, and
thus no reason to do it, but that's game-theory garbage.
As if anyone is that logical. I don't make my bed for the
sake of others; I make it because I can't not.

Until Lydia started regularly sleeping over, and eventually moved in with me, I assumed that my attentiveness
to bed neatness was just this side of the anal-to-anarchic
spectrum. She made her own bed, if not *quite* as well as I
did, so I assumed we were mostly on the same page. But
then, one Sunday morning in my bedroom, as we lolled
about looking at our phones and thinking about what to
make for breakfast, I lifted the comforter above us and
shook it out and smoothed it down, so it lay flat and even
on both sides.

"Katie . . ." Lydia asked. "Are you making the bed?"

"I was just tidying," I said. I hadn't been thinking; it
was purely reflex.

"You are. You're making the bed with us in it."

I said nothing, and she used her foot to flick up the
corner of the comforter at the end of the bed. Coinciden-
tally, I got out of bed to heat up some water for coffee, and

on my way back into the room, I pulled the corner down again. Lydia yelped.

A year into our cohabitation, she is used to the way I am about our bed. She agrees that it feels best getting into a bed that's made with the sheets pulled tight, though I suspect it might be the kind of agreeing you do to make someone you love stop talking—the way I say "yes, babe" when I'm reading next to her on the couch while she plays a video game and she asks if I saw the way she stole that guy's treasure right out from under him. My need to make the bed at all costs does not bother Lydia, but thanks to her, it bothers me. All that time I was single I went around thinking I was a normal, together, calm and cool person, but then I started spending all my time with someone else and realized I'm actually a nightmare.

Making my bed is only my favorite example of personal uptightness, perhaps because it's one of the least offensive ones. The moment we've finished eating, I get up to clear my and Lydia's dishes, which often means I ask her to pause the show we're watching or the story she's telling me so I can clean up. This, again, is something she accepts about me, but she is from one of those families that sits around drinking and talking—for hours—after they've finished eating. I can't understand it. At the outside, it takes my family twenty-five minutes to eat dinner. Growing up, dinnertime fell between 5:30 and 6:00, with my mom cooking, serving, and bringing out a Tupperware container of homemade cookies before the last person had finished their meal. I would put the average number of times she gets up from her chair at each meal (to check on the oven, or grab a forgotten utensil, or get another helping for my dad) at four—six if there are guests. For a number of years we prayed first, which took up a little time, but once we collectively gave up our Catholicism, we really got going. There was a little chitchat, of course—we didn't hate one another—but I think we all figured that we lived together, and ate together every night, and how much new information could there really be since the day before? And when one of the people at the table is obviously anxious for the rest of the people to finish eating and put their dishes away so she can finally sit down and stay sitting down, it feels impolite to draw out the proceedings. Never in my life have I considered mealtime an opportunity to relax and be merry. There is an ephemeral joy in the actual eating, but after I'm done, I cannot rest until all signs that I have eaten are erased, and every condiment and utensil is back where it belongs. Evidently, I get this from my mother.

I am ruthless, too, about working out, and schedule many of my days around it. I have never pressed the snooze button in my life; "sleeping in" on a Sunday means 7:30. If my agreement with myself was to do a certain amount of work before the day is over, I cannot and will not end that day without doing that amount of work. If I fail to do any of the things I have decided I am meant to do on a given day, I am overwhelmed by guilt, and for me, guilt feels far worse than expending the also-sometimes-unpleasant effort it takes to get up and work out and write and eat and clean up after myself as I go. For me the path of least resistance is doing the most I possibly can. And because this is the sort of behavior that is consistently rewarded by pretty much everyone—by parents at home, by teachers in school, by bosses at work—it's easy to sustain the belief that my way of doing things is the most correct one. Or, it used to be.

Something I noticed early about Lydia is that she is open to the possibility that each new person she meets could become her new best friend. When we first met she was working as a general manager of a bagel shop across the street from my apartment, and when she had an early shift on the weekends I'd walk across the street to see her. She would make me an egg sandwich (egg, cheese, avocado, and berry jam—which I balked at, until I tried it), and I would eat it at the counter, eavesdropping while she chatted with customers and the men who came by to deliver eggs and milk and cream cheese. She knew everyone's name and order—something that had always embarrassed me when I was the customer being remembered, until I started spying on Lydia's customers and saw how happy they were to see her, their very own bagel lady, who knew exactly what they wanted.

I thought I was friendly with the men who work at the bodegas and delis in our neighborhood until I started going into the same ones with Lydia. I would say hi, how are you, and thank you, but with Lydia, they had entire comedy routines. For a while we competed over the affections of the guy at our favorite corner store by comparing the things he gave us for free—for me, a banana; for her, a three-dollar granola bar—until it became clear that I would never win. He likes me more now that he knows to associate me with Lydia, but he still likes her best, and I understand why. I've grown more chatty with him since seeing him interact with Lydia, but she was that warm from the start.

None of this is to say that Lydia herself tells me that I am flawed, or need fixing. She thinks I'm so great it's mystifying. Rather, it is that being around her all the time highlights those less attractive things about myself that weren't so glaring when I was single, the way you see your house with fresh eyes the first time you invite a new person into it. It was easier to think I was friendly before I knew Lydia. It was easier to believe I was the most loyal person on Earth before I actually met her. I think I'm pretty nice, but in the middle of the night, if Lydia turns toward me and presses her knee into my back, and I wake up and push it away, she says "Sorry, baby," pats my butt, and turns around again, all in her sleep. When she has PMS, it makes her love me *more*. I am nice, but I am not *that* nice.

When she moved in, Lydia started leaving clothes on the floor. There is always a pile next to the bed—usually, her pajamas, a couple of sweatshirts, the socks she takes off before she slips into bed every night, her shoes. She has a habit, when she comes home after work, of walking straight into our bedroom with her coat and shoes and backpack still on, lying facedown on the bed, and staying there, looking at her phone, for twenty minutes up to an hour. I used to ask her if it wouldn't be more comfortable to take all that extraneous stuff off first so she can really relax, but she's done it this way since she was eight, and it drove her mom nuts, too, so I gave up. If she is somehow able to relax with her coat and shoes and backpack on, I figure I should let her, even knowing that, eventually, those shoes and socks and other layers will accumulate alongside the bed. Sometimes they are arranged in such a way it appears as if she's been Raptured.

This little mountain of bedside clothing goes against everything I value in bed presentation. I wouldn't say my bedrooms have ever been pristine (I am a stacker of books, a perpetual shover of crap into whatever drawers I have available), but they have always appeared tidy. The dust and the magazine piles have been obscured by the main point of pride: the singular neatness of the bed and the floor around it. What good are hospital corners when you have to walk over a pair of tennis shoes and a flannel button-down to turn down the covers? I find this habit of hers mildly aggravating, and more than a little perplexing, given that the hamper is only two feet away from the bed. It doesn't look quite as perfect to me now as it did before I met her. But I like it better now anyway. It isn't just my bed anymore; it's ours.

17

TRUE LOVE

In the first few months of my relationship with Lydia, I kept track—accidentally—of the number of days between our arguments. In my mind I saw it as one of those "days without injury" boards kept in dangerous workplaces: every time we argued (for any length of time, about anything), I reset the calendar to zero. Our average number of fight-free days seemed to be about six or seven, and as I approached the latest record I'd grow uneasy, waiting for it. After a few such weeks I called my mom to ask if she thought this was normal. She told me that when she and my dad first started dating, they would get in a fight every Wednesday. "It was the weirdest thing," she said. It wasn't like these fights were about anything serious, and each Tuesday she'd think they were in the clear, but then Wednesday would roll around, and they'd argue. I should have found comfort in this (they have been happily married for more than thirty-five years), but I didn't, really. My mom and dad at that time were nineteen and twenty, respectively. I was ten years older than she was then, and apparently believed there was an age at which you mature out of the ability to have stupid arguments about nothing. Twenty-six, maybe. That sounded about right.

Our fourth month together was particularly difficult. Toward the end of it we took a ten-day trip to California. For us, this was much too long a trip to take that early on in a relationship, but we did not know that when we booked it. We did not think about how much family time would be involved or how little free time, how much shuttling across the state we'd have to do, how much time we'd have together without respite. We thought: *romance!* We planned to spend our first full day of the trip in Yosemite, which is probably Lydia's favorite place in the world. On the drive up, early that morning, we got in an argument. About what, who can say. Mostly, I think, we just hadn't figured out how to be fully at ease around each other yet. It soon became a gorgeous day—it had snowed the day before, and the sun broke through the clouds over the Curry Village ice rink while Lydia skated and I stood off to the side, taking pictures and whimpering about my sore ankles. The setting could not have been more romantic, and I could not have been more grumpy.

Over the next few days we hung out with her extended family at Pismo Beach, where a couple dozen of her sister's in-laws all camp out in RVs every Thanksgiving. At night we stayed at the nearby Madonna Inn, where Lydia had booked us a room for my birthday. There she also bought me a pink champagne cake that remains the best cake I have ever eaten in my life. We drove to San Diego, where Lydia grew up, and we stayed in her mom's house. The first night we went out to the local lesbian bar, and the second night, when Lydia wanted to meet another home-town friend for catch-up drinks, I did the smartest thing I did the whole trip, and stayed back. Her mom made us veggie burgers and we ate them at her kitchen counter while she told me which friends of Lydia's she liked and which ones she didn't. I fell asleep before Lydia got home, but woke up to her gently sliding my legs out from under the comforter to pull my socks off my feet, and wondered how she knew I was too hot.

It took a long time for me to let these sort of gestures— and the regularity with which we did them for each other, instinctively—make me feel uncomplicatedly good. At the beginning I was so preoccupied with conflict avoid-ance that conflict was all I had space to keep track of. I was so obsessed with our relationship's potential for fail-ure that I weighted each day with the worst of my expec-tations. The proportion of time we have gotten along has always far outweighed the time we haven't, but you wouldn't have known it from the way I behaved. While Lydia, with her ten-plus years of relationship experience, was able to look at our disagreements and recognize them as minor or typical, I had no frame of reference, and treated every clash like a catastrophe. I had spent so much time feeling certain I knew myself better than other peo-ple did, because I was single and always had been, but now that I wasn't, I realized how little I knew about being myself with someone else.

I wish I could say I was an angel the rest of the trip to California, that we got along swimmingly from there on out. But it took more time than that. The fact is that, three days later, I grew so agitated and overwhelmed on a trip to Disneyland that I made Lydia leave me behind in New Orleans Square. We went with her mom, sister, brother-in-law, and niece, and it started out fine. The attendant at the gate gave me two buttons to wear on my jean jacket: one because it was my first time at Disneyland and another because it was my birthday. We stood in line for Mr. Toad's Wild Ride for an hour, and then for the Haunted Mansion for an hour, and then we took a break to eat popcorn from a ten-dollar promotional reindeer basket.

But at some point all the claustrophobia of Fantasyland and the anxiety of the trip came to a head, and I decided I needed a break to sit on something that wouldn't move. Lydia did not want to just sit (there was only so much time left in the day), but she didn't want to leave me behind, either. But I insisted, in a semi-dramatic "just leave me here to die" sort of way, so she walked off to find her family, and I sat at a little plastic table and called my mom and cried. I was still on the phone looking down at the table to hide my tears when a funnel cake in the shape of Mickey Mouse's head was slid under my nose on a paper plate. I looked up and saw the older man in a blue-striped Disney uniform who'd been sweeping the tables around me. He gave me a small smile, and resumed sweeping. I wondered if he had seen my birthday button, too, or just that I was alone, crying on the phone in Disneyland. Was mine the first-ever Mickey Mouse funnel cake given freely out of pity? Thinking about this made me start crying again, but eventually, I knew, it would be funny. I ate one of Mickey's powdered-sugar ears and carried the rest over to It's a Small World so that when Lydia and her family came out of the ride they would find me there waiting with funnel cake to share.

After one of our early arguments, I was talking to Rylee on the phone, trying to get her to tell me either that my relationship was perfect or that it was so awful I should end it. Just as I do not wish to die whenever I seek confirmation of a suspected brain tumor or a faulty heart, I never really *wanted* to break up with Lydia. I wanted certainty.

Rather than suggest I break up with my girlfriend because we'd had an argument (which is probably what I would have done to her when we were younger and every one of my friend's boyfriends seemed disposable), Rylee did what good best friends do and called me out. "You *like* to argue," she said. "It's part of your personality." Well, I *never*. But if I wouldn't have put it that way myself, I can't in good faith say that she is wrong. She and I used to fight all the time, and hard. We didn't bicker, or butt heads; we got along great when we weren't making each other cry. Other people might have let a lot of those grievances go, but conflict avoidance makes me crazy. When a long-term relationship is the goal, I can't see how stewing in one's bad feelings is more productive or less scary than saying them aloud. And Rylee and I always knew we wanted to be friends for a very long time. We cared for each other immensely, but it took time to learn to do it right. Our friend Colleen used to say our fights were about how much we loved each other.

It is like that when I fight with Lydia. It is never about a betrayal of trust, or a failure to care. It is usually about our frustration at not having figured each other out yet. It's my impatience for her to know me completely, and vice versa. For a while I genuinely believed this was something one could actually achieve.

It wasn't until I was in a relationship of my own that I realized how little I understood of other people's. For example, I used to take people's social media posts about their boyfriends or girlfriends pretty much at face value. When women I knew posted pictures of themselves with their boyfriends above captions like "love of my life" and "always happy to spend the day with this one" and "#tbt to when we met and right away I knew he was the one," I may have rolled my eyes, but I also kind of took them literally. I believed in finding The One and knowing without a doubt that they are The One. Despite all the times I'd counseled friends through fights with their boyfriends, I believed that it was possible to find someone you simply do not fight with. And when people described someone as the love of their life, or said they couldn't wait to spend the rest of their life with someone, I assumed it was because they'd gained access to a higher plane of consciousness reserved for only those who are *truly* in love.

Now that I know what it feels like to be in love, I see these captions and clichés for what they really are: mostly bullshit. Not bullshit in the total fabrication sense, but in the way you fill the last page and a half of a college essay due in two hours. Bullshit in a way that gets at the heart of the matter but in a way that is too tidy, and leaves a lot left unsaid. I do not mean to say that the women I knew as girls in high school do not really love the men they are married to, but I have to believe they sometimes hate them a little bit, too. I have to believe that when they post something about "five years of utter bliss" on their anniversaries on Facebook, they are being generous, and a little forgetful. I need to believe these things because if I don't I will drive myself crazy. I am too malleable and too suggestible not to take pat romantic clichés to heart, to file them away and call them to mind when I am feeling even a hint of uncertainty or inadequacy. It's why I couldn't stand to read letters in relationship advice columns the full first year Lydia and I were together, no matter how little the situations described in their headlines had to do with my own. When I was single, reading relationship columns made me feel smug for not being in what was almost always clearly a terrible relationship. Reading them in the infancy of my own relationship only made me worry that I could one day be just like all those letter writers, clueless as to just how terrible my relationship really was. It took me twenty-eight years to realize I wanted to be with a woman; what other secrets might I have buried inside me?

Despite all my fears, something clicked into place after a year with Lydia, if not the perfect conviction I once

18

PARIS

I have wanted to go to Paris for as long as I can remember. Like wanting a horse of one's own, like wanting bangs, wanting to go to Paris is a phase the average girl goes through at least once, at least before she is old enough to develop a real personality. I grew out of everything else, but the amount I wanted to go to Paris never wavered. This, at times, embarrassed me. When people asked me where I most wanted to travel, I'd say "Oh, probably Paris," an apologetic confession. Nobody *really* cares where you want to travel next unless it happens to be the same place they want to travel next, but I felt judged for having failed, in nearly thirty years, to come up with anything unique. There were other places I wanted to go that were less popular an answer than Paris, but none of them were fixed. The last time I'd been out of the country was when I was in Spain in 2008, and since then, whatever space I had in my brain for plotting world travels was dedicated, single-mindedly, to France.

My interest in Paris was mostly due to abstract concepts like "chicness" and "elegance." I did not picture seeing the Eiffel Tower or the Louvre so much as I did walking down narrow, cobbled roads with a baguette tucked under my arm. I was pretty sure that people didn't really wear berets anymore, but I still imagined women in striped shirts with silk scarves tied around their necks. I imagined twinkling lights and swelling violin music and a mixture of scenes from *Sex and the City* and *Amélie*.

When I was a teenager and into my early twenties, Paris was also my top choice among potential honeymoon locations. But by my mid-twenties, I realized I was not going to be getting married anytime soon, and would need another reason to go to Paris if I wanted to make it there before who knows when. Rylee and I talked about going together some October as a sort of midpoint celebration between our birthdays, which fall in September (hers) and November (mine). But every time we tried to pick a year, there was some other trip or massive expense getting in the way. One year Rylee went to Turkey; the next, I moved to New York. We never felt like we had enough money. Eventually we decided we should go for our thirtieth birthdays. It was more meaningful that way anyway, and surely by the time we were thirty we would have healthy savings accounts set aside for this sort of thing. We agreed on this plan as firmly as you can about something far-off and big like a ten-day trip to Paris. Rylee promised me that even if she had a boyfriend or a husband by then, she would take the trip with me and me alone. It did not occur to either of us that I make a similar promise; there was no need. I was always the one willing and able and full of free time, ready to squeeze myself into whatever windows my friends could pry open.

And yet, by the time thirty was approaching, there I was, in a relationship. And the longer Lydia and I were together, the harder it became to imagine taking a trip to the most romantic city in the world with someone else, especially over a holiday, or on my birthday. I wanted to go to Paris with her more than I wanted to go with Rylee, and realizing that made me feel so guilty my chest hurt. But then Lydia and I decided we couldn't go to Chiara's wedding, and decided we probably couldn't go to France, either, and Rylee booked a trip to the Ukraine, and then it didn't matter anymore, because *nobody* was going to Paris.

But then Chiara talked me into buying a pair of plane tickets, even though I'd told her I couldn't go to her wedding because I couldn't afford it. We were talking over Gchat as usual, and I said I was sad I wasn't going to get to follow through on my great Paris plan.

why can't you still go? wrote Chiara.

money and time?

i'm really a believer in the spontaneous "just do it before you think about it too much," she wrote.

cause you'll never regret it and you make money back.

Basically, she said: Sometimes, you just have to go and figure the rest out later.

So I set up some flight alerts, and a couple of weeks later found a great price on direct flights from New York to Paris over the Thanksgiving holiday (and, not incidentally, my birthday). I texted Lydia for her confirmation, which arrived in a burst of enthusiastic, capitalized, spelling-error-ridden messages, and put the plane tickets on my credit card. I was going to celebrate my thirtieth birthday in Paris after all—just not in the way I'd originally planned it, or with the person with whom I'd originally planned it. But sometimes plans change, and perhaps someday I will learn to be okay with that.

On our first full day in Paris, I stormed away from Lydia in the Louvre. I did not go far—the Louvre is a large museum, and my phone didn't work particularly well in there, and even though Lydia was now my enemy, I did not want to get separated from her in a foreign country where I did not speak the language. So while she sat on an alcoved bench next to a window in English paintings, I huffed my way to the opposite end of Spanish paintings, one gallery over. I sat down on my own bench, next to a young man listening to an audio guide on headphones. I pretended to look at the paintings in front of me, and then swiveled around to pretend to look at the ones behind me, too. What I was actually doing was waiting for Lydia to come find me. The way I envisioned it, she would be slightly panicked, afraid that I had left the museum and was out in the city, alone and Frenchless. I gave it five or six minutes, and then I started to worry that maybe *she* would leave *me* in the museum, so I got up and walked, stupidly, back over to the spot I'd only just left. Lydia was still there.

I have no idea what made us upset with each other that day, apart from the fact that it seems our destiny to become inexplicably irritated with each other on the first day of most trips we take. There must be some kind of vacation curse; either that or I am perpetually damning myself with impossible expectations. You spend all that time saving up and waiting and planning perfect days for your perfect trip, and then one day you're just . . . there. How disappointing, to no longer have the great big adventure in front of you, free to remain hypothetically perfect. How stressful to have to actually go through it.

For a long time I arranged my life as a series of relatively short-term plans. I had a lot of expectations for how things *should* go, but very little imagination as to just how many ways they might. In high school and college and into my twenties, I thought that I should get a boyfriend. I could not have known that my failure to do so would leave all my time and love free for my friends instead, or how it would give me a thicker skin, a better sense of humor, and plenty to write about. I thought I should have sex with a man before I was twenty-five. I did not expect to feel *relieved* to have sex for the first time at twenty-eight, because it would be with a woman, and I'd know for sure why I'd never gotten around to doing what I'd thought I wanted.

Our first day in Paris was mapped out nearly to the minute, and Louvre incident notwithstanding, it was perfectly fine. But the next day, my birthday, Lydia and I decided to spend an hour and a half waiting in freezing rain to get into the Catacombs so that I could celebrate turning thirty among the human skulls. It was not what I would have described had I been asked at fifteen, or even twenty-five, to outline my perfect birthday in Paris. It was better.

Girl #7

Any girl I heard was bisexual, college. College was the closest I've ever come to pure and total boy craziness. Rather than dedicating myself to an unlikely, unrequited crush over a period of one to two years like I had in high school, I liked a new boy every three months. I talked to them, even, and kissed some of them at parties: drunk and pressed against a wall, drunk and sitting on their laps. I was always pleased to be doing it, thinking all the while that I was adding a name and a number to my list, distancing myself (however slightly) from the virginal loser I felt I was. I was never all that into the kissing itself. I wondered if there was supposed to be more to it, but I wasn't sure what that "more" could be. In the cafeteria, where we would recap the previous night's events, I'd hear things that scandalized me. Most notably: that the two sexiest, drunkest girls in our class would sometimes go down on each other in front of this guy we all knew. "I guess they say they're 'bisexual,'" my friend said, rolling her eyes in time with her mocking air quotes. I had a *lot* of questions. I still do.

19

SOMETHING NEW

When my brothers and I were younger the story of how my parents met went like this: my dad saw my mom at the milk machine in the school cafeteria and told the friend sitting next to him that he was going to marry her. They dated for two years, until my mom had graduated, and then my dad proposed to her in a limo. He'd teasingly proposed to her enough times already that my mom said, "Do you mean it this time?" My dad said yes, so she did, too.

The sweetness of this story nearly ruined my life.

Even when I was a kid I thought that twenty-two (or even twenty-four) seemed young, but I still held my parents' relationship trajectory up as the platonic ideal. When I was eighteen I thought, *Well, I have two years to meet him if I want to be on track.* When I was twenty I thought, *Well, I could be twenty-three, that would be fine.* When I was twenty-four I thought, *Dear God, I can't imagine being married* now. But maybe that's only because it was too late for me to mirror my parents, and if I wasn't going to have a love story like theirs I needed to talk myself out of ever having wanted it.

Now that I am thirty, and more actively contemplating marriage, I *truly* cannot imagine having been married for six years already. By the age I am now my mother had given birth to all three of her kids. It is already incomprehensible enough for me to think about what it means to spend the next, say, forty-five years with someone (presuming I'm lucky enough to live until seventy-five)— surely adding another six or seven on top of that would have been pushing it. Now that I am past the age I'd hoped, as a very young person, to be married, I can see clearly that I am who I am, and have accomplished what I have, because I'm not. This is not to say that my parents or anyone who marries younger is necessarily missing out on something essential, but rather that no two paths are the same, and no single path is correct.

Neither are most relationships and marriages exactly as they appear from the outside. For instance, a few years ago, I learned the real circumstances under which my parents first met. My mom and I had gone on a road trip to Montana to visit my youngest brother at school, and something about the unlikely combination of just the three of us hanging out together made us all unusually forthcoming. (It was also on this trip that my mom *finally* admitted to having "tried pot" when she was younger.) I brought up the milk-machine story and my mom told us that was actually the *second* time my dad had seen her.

"What was the first??" I asked.

"Well," she said, "I don't remember."

It turns out that my parents first met not in the cafeteria in broad daylight, but at a frat party at which my mother was blackout drunk. "They had these huge garbage bins they'd cleaned out and filled to the top with rum or something," she said, shrugging, evidently not realizing the impact that the milk-machine story had had on my young psyche. My dad had not, in fact, alighted on my mom (whom I'd imagined in this scene with a halo around her reddish curls) in the cafeteria and fallen in love despite having never met her; he had recognized the cute drunk girl from the party the other night and thought she seemed fun.

This is, I know, a better and much truer story than the one I grew up with. It is still very sweet, but it's also funny, and a little embarrassing. It makes their relationship and their marriage seem less like destiny and more like real life. I still think it's amazing that they found each other and have been happy together for as long as they have. I can understand why my parents left binge drinking out of the version of events they told their small children. Still, I can't help but think that if I'd known the full story sooner, I might have been less hopelessly romantic myself.

When I was in my early twenties, I decided I wanted to be proposed to on the Jumbotron at a Twins game. Like many of the things I have been certain I wanted at various points in my life—like the ten-thousand-dollar Tiffany-cut diamond engagement ring I thought I wanted from ages twelve to twenty-two—this desire is so utterly unrecognizable to me now that I have to imagine I was full of shit. Certainly, I like going to baseball games very much, and true, it makes me swoon to watch other couples get engaged on the screen over left-center field. At that time I also had my heart set on marrying a six-foot-four Midwestern baseball fan (Minnesotan, if at all possible), and so this seemed like a good way to honor our shared heritage and interests. I also love attention, and did not foresee any other circumstance in which some forty thousand people might applaud me at once. But I don't want too much attention for too long, which made the Jumbotron proposal an even better fit—the whole thing would be over in less than two minutes.

In the meantime, I liked telling people I wanted to be proposed to on the Jumbotron because it surprised them. It is a relatively low-maintenance preference, which is not an adjective with which I am typically associated. I am not a person who leaves the house without at least eyebrow pencil and mascara on. I am not the woman who's like, "I'll take whatever's on tap." I have never in my life successfully rolled with the punches. So I liked to think that telling people I wanted to get engaged in a baseball park gave them pause—that it made them think, *Huh, maybe Katie is actually pretty chill.* I did not care about a fancy dinner or a limo or champagne; nor did I care, by then, about the size of the ring. I abandoned Tiffany in favor of laid-backness.

I believe it was my friend Rachel who put me off the

Jumbotron dream. I was twenty-six and had organized a group of friends to go see the Twins play at Yankee Stadium. A few innings in, when the Kiss Cam started up and we waited to see if a proposal would follow, I leaned over to deliver my line: "I kinda want to be proposed to like this, on a Jumbotron."

Rachel turned to me, her eyebrows brought together by disdain. "No, you don't," she said. "That would be awful."

I blinked at her, then turned my eyes back to the screen. The kissing concluded, and when no one asked anyone else to get married, I was relieved. Rachel was . . . right. I did not want to get engaged on a Jumbotron at a baseball park. I did not want my dumb fiancé-to-be kneeling on sticky cement and shouting *"Will you marry me?"* over the roar of forty thousand drunken strangers, rushing through it because there was only so much time before they had to get back to the game. I did not want the pressure of forty thousand people watching my thirty-foot-tall face onscreen to see if they could tell how excited I was, or wasn't. In fact, it was actually quite selfish of him to set me up in this way, knowing I couldn't very well say no with forty thousand people watching. How could I marry someone who clearly did not know me at all? What had I been thinking?

It is delusions like these that make me doubt my ability to read my own mind. I suppose it is possible that my personality genuinely did change, and I was once the type of girl who would have been down with a Jumbotron proposal over beer and Cracker Jack. I suppose it is possible that I did once see myself with the man I pictured on the other end of that proposal, the six-foot-four Minnesotan with a beard. But now that I do not want either of these things, it is hard for me to believe in an earlier me who did. That me is a little like the me who believed in Santa Claus—there is enough documentation of my one-time belief system that I cannot deny its existence, but it embarrasses me now, having fallen for something so obviously untrue. Then again, maybe it's better to be a sucker than a know-it-all; the worst kid in every kindergarten class is the one who just found out that Santa isn't real, and who will not rest until everyone else knows, too.

It was a relief, for a while, pinning my romance-related hopes and dreams on a Tiffany-cut diamond or a Jumbotron engagement. I spent years feeling like I wasn't getting any closer to finding someone to love, and when I needed a break from worrying I never would, I could think about the little things instead. I could assemble the whole scene so that when it finally arrived, some indeterminate number of years into the future, I would be ready.

Last fall, a month before I turned thirty, my younger brother got married. He was twenty-seven, and his new wife, twenty-four. I'd met his fiancée only a few times, and liked her as much as I possibly could given the information I had. But she was so young, and he, while not quite as young, is perpetually ten or fifteen years younger than he really is, because he is my little brother. "Isn't this a little fast?" I'd asked my mom. "He's twelve."

I flew home for my brother's wedding as someone who wanted as little to do with weddings as possible. I'd been building up a distaste toward what I liked to refer to as the wedding industrial complex for the past several years, instilled by reading Rebecca Mead and strengthened by hate-watching *Say Yes to the Dress* on TLC. On Facebook I witnessed girls I went to high school with throwing identical bridal showers and bachelorette parties and wearing their identical, strapless, beaded white gowns. I started hearing, through the grapevine, the horror stories—a girl I knew in college (a girl I *thought* I knew) had reportedly insisted that her shorter-hair bridesmaids get wedding-day extensions for the sake of photogenic sameness. I thought the "ugly bridesmaid dress" thing was an overstated and outdated joke until my friends started having to buy them. At one time a ten-thousand-dollar engagement ring didn't seem *so* crazy to me, and then I found out there were people I knew paying that much for a dress they'd wear once. That there were people I knew paying twenty or thirty thousand dollars for their weddings while asking guests to buy them eighty-dollar pans and ten-dollar plates seemed absurd and borderline offensive. Why not tone down the party a little and buy the goddamn plates yourself?

Throughout this period I was, of course, single.

The economics of it all still get under my skin. There are things we do and buy in service of weddings that we do not and would not do for anything else. If your friend invited you to a ten-thousand-dollar, two-day party across the country to celebrate her new job, and asked you to help pay for her new work wardrobe, you'd be like "Uhh-hhhh??" As far as I can tell, your wedding is the only time in your life that most people will be willing to drop everything and spend anything for you. No wonder that the pressure and the power goes to some people's heads.

It was this Miss Buzzkill Scrooge persona that led me, in part, to RSVP "no" to Chiara's wedding a month before my brother's, and while my regret over that decision had chastened me, there was still a small knot of wedding resentment roiling in my belly by the time I flew back to Minnesota. I expected to get through the wedding largely unaffected—not unmoved by love, or my brother's evident adulthood, or the circle of life more broadly, but with my so-called principles more or less intact. I expected to get back to New York feeling as sure I did not want a wedding for myself as I was when I left it.

But goddammit: the wedding was lovely. It was held outside under a gray sky that stopped raining just in time. My brother's best friend from college officiated, and he cried during his speech, which made the rest of us cry, too. I stood on my brother's side, wearing a suit, because he and his fiancée had decided the members of the wedding party should stand on the side of the person they knew first. The bride and groom wrote their own vows, both of which mentioned their pet rabbits. The ceremony took all of fifteen minutes. It was conventional, but it was personal, too. It was, I think, what most people are going for when they plan a wedding.

I have not been to many weddings as an adult, yet. Just two of my closest friends are married, and none of the others are even engaged. We are statistically behind the curve. Ever since my friends started getting invited to four or five weddings a year I have been waiting for the same thing to happen to me, but it hasn't. I listened to friends and co-workers list off their summer wedding travel schedules and considered myself fortunate in much the same way I felt lucky when, at fifteen, I still hadn't gotten my period. But now, having gone to my brother's wedding, I am cautiously looking forward to this era in my life. I am sure I will get stressed and annoyed about the money, and I am sure I will still find it hard to be sympathetic to some of the things brides tend to worry about. But then, I hope I will remember how it felt to be there that day, watching my brother marry the woman he loves, and recognize it as a privilege. I hope I am so lucky as to see my youngest brother and my other best friends marry people they love, too. I don't know if this means I am maturing, or getting marginally less judgmental, or if it's just that I am in love now, too, and therefore a hypocrite.

In Paris, standing below the lit-up Eiffel Tower, Lydia got down on one knee, and asked me if I could wait a second while she tied her shoe. It was the second time she'd pulled this particular prank, which I think is pushing it. It is probably pushing it to attempt it once. It's also a joke that is only "funny" if both people know the person doing the fake proposing intends to actually propose at some point in the future. I knew from the outset that she was pretending because I had made her promise not to propose to me in Paris; it was a little too early, and a little too cliché. Even still, for just a fraction of a second, I panicked, and then I yelped "Don't!!!" I didn't have enough time to think about what I would have said if she'd really been asking; it was only enough for me to register that my resolve was being tested, and I *would not bend.* I am not surprised that my best and sharpest reflex works in service of my stubbornness, but I am disappointed. If only I could have followed the ball (any kind of ball) as efficiently as I can say *no,* my athletic career might have gone a lot differently.

To Lydia's credit, she was not bothered for very long by my yelling *"Don't"* at the idea of her proposing to me. She is not, in fact, bothered by very much for very long, a trait I find baffling and occasionally irritating as well as incredibly admirable. For a while now she has made it clear that she would like to marry me. The first time she said so, I felt anxious and mystified. How could she possibly know that, already? How did she know she wouldn't change her mind, or grow to hate me, before the year was out? But the more time that went by, the less crazy an idea our eventual engagement seemed.

Somewhere in there I started looking at engagement rings again. Not from Tiffany, which is no longer my style, and not for ten thousand dollars, or anywhere close. I am too aware now of how much money that is, and how far it can go, to want it spent on a single object I might not like as much in ten years as I do now. Sometimes I send pictures of ones I like to Lydia, or tag her in the comments beneath a picture of a pretty ring I see on Instagram. Just to "see what she says." Much to my chagrin, I have become a hint dropper. I am not ready for her to ask me yet. Nor am I positive that that's the way it should happen. Sometimes I think I might like to be the one to ask her. Most of my romantic life has been defined by passively waiting for something to happen *to* me: to be asked

out, to be kissed, to be seduced, to be made someone's
girlfriend, someone's wife. When I came out I took hold
of my own life and yanked it somewhere new. If and when
I get married, I don't expect it will be because I "know," at
least not in the permanent, incontestable way people
imply when they say things like that about those they
marry. I could die waiting for absolute certainty. I have
unsubscribed from that particular fairy tale. When I
marry, I hope it is with the expectation that I will occasionally fall short, and so will she—and with enough trust
to believe that we will love each other anyway, as best we
can, for as long as we can. The rest is just details.

EPILOGUE

Most of the time, when my girlfriend and I pass another queer couple on the street, the four of us exchange a brief but knowing glance. If we aren't already holding hands or touching in some way, Lydia will sometimes put a hand around my waist, and I swear that at least half the time the other couple does something similar. Without physical evidence one can certainly conjecture as to the nature of the relationship between two women walking together, and I have gotten much better at differentiating between friends and girlfriends. But same-sex relationships are not presumed the way straight ones are, so when we want to be sure that someone else sees us for what we are, we engage in light PDA. I don't know why, exactly; in most cases these are people we never meet or see again. I don't know for sure that what is going through my mind is going through theirs. Historically, I am prone to overthinking. But I think there's something going on there, some small reflexive ping of recognition. I never notice how much I am missing that kind of connection until it's happening, and then it's over.

Maybe because my same-sex relationship is barely two years old, and I have been out for only slightly longer than that, I forget that what I am is unusual. I have been so extraordinarily lucky. My friends and my family and everyone I knew accepted my coming-out almost immediately and with very few questions. I live in a city where it is not unusual to see other queer couples on a daily basis, and where I feel relatively comfortable displaying my sexuality in public. It is only when we travel elsewhere, outside New York, that I remember that there are people who find me, and my relationship, disgusting.

I spent so, so many years worrying that I would never have a real relationship. And when I finally had one, I expected, naïvely, that I would no longer feel left out. Finally I had the thing that everyone had been telling me I needed, directly and indirectly, for twenty-eight years. And to some extent, I do feel more accepted as a thirty-year-old queer woman with a girlfriend than I did as a single, supposedly straight, and sexless twenty-seven-year-old. I have the frame of reference for couple-y concerns and in-jokes that were beyond the range of my empathy when I was alone. I can give relationship advice with marginally more authority than before. But when it comes to looking to our culture for authentic, relatable stories about queer women, it is still a fucking slog. Thank God for *Carol* because before it, queer women characters existed mostly to tempt and to die. After *Carol* (A.C.) this is still true, but at least we have that one bright spot.

It's not that I think TV and movies gave me very much in the way of realism or relatability before, when I was a young woman who considered herself straight. Then, though, I saw the hope of something that *could* happen to me. I could be awkward and kind of clumsy and bad at dating, and still, one day, a man would find me charming and sexy. That I was a journalist seemed like a good start—pretty much half of all romantic comedies involve a woman finding love as a result of covering the fluffy story their bitchy boss wants them to cover instead of *real* news like they wanted. There was very little available in terms of what to expect after landing the man, but by a certain point that was all I had the energy to care about anyway.

Better than TV and movies were books and magazine articles and, best of all, relationship-advice columns. At some point in my twenties it became very easy to find novels about disaffected young women who are mostly unhappy with their boyfriends, and that gave me comfort when I was lonely—*At least I'm not missing out on much,* I thought. I never could find stories by women who'd never had boyfriends, but I could find ones by women who had just been tragically dumped by theirs and were therefore in *almost* the same position as I was. In magazines and blogs and advice columns and music I could find women near enough my age and circumstances that I felt we had something in common because, if nothing else, the language fit. They'd been hurt by *him,* they didn't understand why *he* didn't feel the same way; there was this guy, and they wanted him to be their boyfriend. Even if none of the finer details matched, that basic narrative fit mine.

But this is all easy to say now. If I could tell my younger self "You don't know how good you had it," I know she would roll her eyes.

As a young person I thought I was conscious of heteronormative language and just how widely it ranged, but I had no idea. I remember getting dutifully angry the first time I saw a store advertising women's "boyfriend jeans," but I absorbed an infinite number of marketing emails filled with *him*'s and *he*'s and *his*'s without notice. Now, though, I see it and hear it always. It is all-encompassing: every commercial, every store's website, every women's magazine cover, every movie poster, every TV show. Recently I found myself getting upset with a true-crime podcast host because he said something about it being tragic that the young woman who'd been murdered hadn't lived to have her first boyfriend. It was included among a list of life markers and achievements—he wasn't being sexist, really—but it was jarring to me. I was like, *Um, what if she'd wanted to date girls?* Then I remembered that I was listening to a murder podcast and the eventual sexual preference of the teenage victim was kind of beside the point.

I am probably the seven-millionth gay person to point out how much it sucks to feel constantly erased by something as tiny as pronouns in advertising. I am, as ever, late to the party. I don't even really care about boyfriend jeans, and I don't really mind correcting someone who assumes the person I'm dating is a man. Statistically speaking, they are making the safer guess. I like being different, usually, and I like belonging to a minority community. I like being *queer*. But I feel left out and lonely sometimes, like I did before. Apparently that is part of the deal of being alive.

My points of connection with other humans feel rarer now that I am out, and when they do come along I am prone to emotional outbursts. One day late last summer, late enough that it should have been fall but wasn't close to feeling that way, Lydia met me at work for lunch. She usually has one weekday off per week, and will sometimes use the middle of it taking the subway to and from the city all so we can sit together and eat falafel in the park for twenty minutes. On that particular day I was looking to extend my work break for as long as I thought I could get away with it, so after we finished lunch we walked around looking for a Mister Softee truck. By the time we found one (having ignored a half dozen impostors called things like Sir Frosty and Mr. Cone) we were running short on time, so we got our rainbow-sprinkled cones and started speed-walking back toward my office. We hustled through a giant group of teenagers milling around outside their school, annoyed at them for taking up the whole side-walk, until we heard one of them yell, "You two make a great couple!" I turned to yell "Thanks!" and saw a young woman with an intricately shaved short haircut and baggy men's sweatpants looking back and smiling. I made it around the corner before I cried into my ice cream cone. Lydia and I hadn't been holding hands, or even walking particularly close together, as I am both a much faster walker and more afraid to be caught playing hooky from work. And yet, this girl had seen us, and known.

. . .

It doesn't happen as often anymore, but occasionally I still get emails from young women who have just read my first book. Usually it is obvious that they do not know that I have since come out as gay. (Why would they? There was no press release, and fortunately most people do not spend as much time on Twitter as I do.) When I write back to thank them and tell them how much it means, always, to hear that someone can relate, I feel like I am being somehow deceptive. Even when they do not ask what has happened in my life since, which is most often the case, I still feel like I'm lying by omission, letting them believe that my life has unfolded the way they expect given the course set by that book. I'm not embarrassed—if someone asks, I will answer—rather, it's that I don't want to be responsible for ruining anyone's source of comfort. Because while it is true that some of the young women who read my first book and feel the same will eventually realize that they are queer, most of them probably won't. Their stories will diverge from mine. And I am afraid that once they realize that we are *not* the same, they will no longer relate to me, and they will lose interest.

Sometimes I find myself getting angry with hypothetical strangers for deciding they have nothing more to say to me, and no more interest in hearing from me, now that I am no longer the longtime single girl who wants a boyfriend. I am aware that this is a waste of time on a number of levels. For one, it makes me madder to imagine someone not liking me than it does when I find out that a real person actually does not like me. I am not very bothered by the idea of someone not liking me from start to finish; it is the idea that someone who once liked me a lot could eventually stop that keeps me having plenty to talk about in therapy.

Part of being a memoirist or an essayist or whatever you want to call it (but please choose something that makes me sound respectable) is that your relatability and your likability become part of your job. For women writers, anyway. I can afford, in my private life, to be a bit uptight and closed-off and shy, so long as I am fine with having a reputation for resting bitchface and receiving invitations to very few of the best parties. But if I want to keep writing books that people buy, and I do, I cannot afford to have you dislike me or find me unrelatable. Now, I know there are plenty of people who bought my first book and very much did not like me. I saw enough multiparagraph reviews of my bad personality on various blogs to get the idea. But I think most of the people who read my first book came out of it liking me all right, and why shouldn't they? In that book I am funny, and self-deprecating, and cheerfully optimistic. I am awkward but not strange. I am single but not too terribly stressed about it. I have crushes on boys that are, for the most part, unrequited. After the book came out someone wrote a review of it that heavily implied that I was, in fact, *too* likable. It is a very fine balance.

If it makes that reviewer feel any better, I am pretty sure I am growing less likable over time. (That's not a brag.) I don't have a lot of evidence to support this; it's just a hunch. I will tell you, though, that most straight men do *not* have much at all to say to you after you make it clear you have no intention of ever sleeping with them. My dating history tells me that men were never my biggest fans, but before I came out, they dropped by from time to time: to say hi, how was your weekend, to make unfunny jokes at me on Twitter, and even, once in a while, to ask me out. There was a modicum of interest. In my first book I referred to myself as an anthropomorphized Bermuda Triangle; as in, most men aren't aware I exist, and those that are can't often be bothered to visit. Let me tell you, a Bermuda Triangle has nothing on a lesbian.

So there goes almost half the population. Not that I'm complaining, but you do notice.

Toward the end of high school I had this epiphany that maybe some of the people with whom I'd gone to high school hadn't liked me as much as I assumed they did. I was at some party, one of the few involving alcohol I attended as a senior with white-knuckled terror. A friend of mine—or so I thought—was exaggeratedly and performatively drunk, the way you get when you are eighteen and mixing vodka with Sprite. She hooked an arm around my neck and told me, "You know, I didn't really like you until this year."

This was a girl I'd been nominally friends with since middle school. We had gone trick-or-treating together. When we had the same lunch period, we ate at the same table in the cafeteria. I had been to her house. And while we had never been especially close, and she was known in our group for being fickle with her attention, it had never occurred to me to think she didn't like me at least as much as she liked any of the rest of us. The whole thing set me off on an existential crisis. I was not popular in high school and certainly not before it, but I never walked around my school feeling unliked. I knew myself to be a fairly kind, thoughtful, and loyal person, and so I assumed that everyone else thought of me that way, too.

I realized then that I'd been operating on the assumption that because I wasn't really aware of anyone who didn't like me, most people must. I had spent nearly eighteen years of my life failing to consider a third possibility: that most people did not care about me one way or the other. To me this seemed far worse than finding out someone hated me. When I was sixteen someone told me that Melissa B. from Spanish class hated my guts, so I simply started hating her back. I still don't know why, or if it was even true, but I have considered her a low-level enemy ever since. Antipathy, I can deal with. I like myself enough to get more mad than hurt when someone decides they cannot stand me. It's ambivalence that really gets under my skin. And the older I get, the more I am aware of it.

Age itself, I'm sure, is no small part of it—there is only so much time in the day, and I do not want to waste any of it alongside someone or several someones I don't much care for. I can't blame anyone for prioritizing similarly. Five or so years ago I had more friends than I do today, and I think that is probably true for most people over the age of thirty.

The sad part is that I am positive I am a better person today than I was five years ago, and much better still than five years before that. Surely most people improve as they get older. And yet, it is never again as easy to surround ourselves with friends as when we are at our youngest and our stupidest. In theory, I should be easier to like than ever before. But my world seems so much smaller than it used to be. I worry I was born with only a finite amount of likability in me, and I wasted too much of it on prior selves.

When I was a teenager I'd lie awake in bed for hours, legs in the air, feet pointed and then flexed, trying to stretch through the dull aching in my calves that came as a consequence of a rather sudden growth spurt. My whole life I'd thought of myself as short, until, seemingly out of nowhere, I was tall. Coming out has been a bit like this. More than two years later I am still stretching, reaching for something solid enough to stand on.

I cannot change anything about the trajectory of my past, and if I were given the opportunity, I am not sure that I would. But I suspect that some of the things I have only recently learned, at twenty-eight and twenty-nine and thirty, are things most people figure out much earlier. All that time I spent feeling righteous about my so-called conviction-based singleness, I had no idea how much work I had left to do. Being alone throughout my adolescence and young adulthood made me strong in some ways, but left me unchallenged in others, too. Some of the friends I judged for their back-to-back boyfriends have more than a decade's worth of the kind of interpersonal experience I am only now starting to accumulate. To make myself feel better when I was single I told myself that I would come out ahead in the end, wiser and happier for having spent so much time by myself.

But true and lasting love is not a reward you get for

good behavior, and definitely not one you get for self-righteousness. There are a million ways to arrive there, and most of them look an awful lot like luck. There is no universal secret to getting it, and though I am sure I will keep looking, just in case, I'm pretty sure there isn't one to keeping it, either. The only way I know how to find love is the one that worked for me, and that one took twenty-eight-and-a-half years. The amount of time I spent waiting may not be so long in the grand scheme of things, but it wasn't that long ago that I felt I'd been waiting forever. I waited until I couldn't stand to wait anymore, and then, finally, I tried something different.

ACKNOWLEDGMENTS

I want to thank my personal dream team—my editor, Sara Weiss, and my agent, Allison Hunter, both of whom I adore.

I also want to thank Anna Sale, whose interest in my story encouraged other people to take interest, too.

Thanks to the many queer women who made me feel welcome when I wasn't sure where I stood, especially Sheila, Valerie, Lindsay, Mackenzie, Chris, Shannon, Sally, and Chloe. Thanks to Tegan and Sara for their music and their haircuts.

Thanks to Rylee, for taking my many exploratory comings-out in stride. Thanks to Chiara, for the conviction and the swiftness of her text messages. Thanks to Arianna, for always knowing exactly what I mean. And thanks to Rachel, for her killer editorial instincts and her generosity.

Thanks to my family, for supporting me, loving me, and working tirelessly to sell my books to every stranger they meet.

And finally—thank you, Lydia, for taking my hand.

KATIE HEANEY is the author of two memoirs, *Never Have I Ever* and *Would You Rather?,* and the novel *Dear Emma.* She also co-authored the novel *Public Relations* with Arianna Rebolini. She lives in Brooklyn, where she works as a freelance writer.

katieheaney.com
Facebook.com/KTHeaney
Twitter: @KTHeaney
Instagram: @katieheaney

ABOUT THE TYPE

This book was set in Garamond, a typeface originally designed by the Parisian type cutter Claude
Garamond (c. 1500–61). This version of Garamond
was modeled on a 1592 specimen sheet from the
Egenolff-Berner foundry, which was produced from
types assumed to have been brought to Frankfurt by
the punch cutter Jacques Sabon (c. 1520–80).

Claude Garamond's distinguished romans and
italics first appeared in *Opera Ciceronis* in 1543–44.
The Garamond types are clear, open, and elegant.